THE A TO Z OF ABSOLUTELY EVERYTHING

PETER COREY

A REALLY CRUCIAL GUIDE TO LIFE

Peter Corey

Illustrated by Martin Brown

Hippo Books
Scholastic Publications Limited
London

Scholastic Publications Ltd,
10 Earlham Street, London WC2H 9RX, UK

Scholastic Inc,
730 Broadway, New York, NY 10003, USA

Scholastic Tab Publications Ltd,
123 Newkirk Road, Richmond Hill,
Ontario L4C 3G5, Canada

Ashton Scholastic Pty Ltd,
PO Box 579, Gosford, New South Wales,
Australia

Ashton Scholastic Ltd,
165 Marua Road, Panmure, Auckland 6,
New Zealand

First published by Scholastic Publications Ltd., 1990

ISBN 0 590 76314 8

Made and printed by Cox & Wyman, Reading, Berks
Photoset by Goodfellow & Egan Ltd, Cambridge

10 9 8 7 6 5 4 3 2 1

ABOUT THIS BOOK

The journey through life can be very hazardous indeed. Especially the bit you're on now. And it doesn't get any easier. Why, sometimes it's more difficult than trying to work out a bus timetable, or follow the plot of *Home and Away*. Of course, if you need advice, you can always *ask* somebody, but how do you know if they know any more about life than you do? I suppose to a degree it depends who you ask. I mean, if you ask the old man lying in the corner, apparently trying to drink a brown paper bag, you'll probably get the answer: "Thbm jbiuym,m ghgrs/.;jvctrd6543", which may or may not be right. It's a problem, isn't it?

Or, at least, it *was* – until now. This book contains all the answers, even though I don't know what the questions are. It is crammed with facts, advice and opinions, some of which may even be true! Much of the information is designed to prepare you for the Big Harsh World beyond the comparative safety of home and the comparative gloom of school. We live in a consumer society, so there's plenty of consumer advice, whatever that is. We live in a pretty silly society too, and that fact hasn't gone unnoticed. In this book you'll find everything you need to know to prevent you being ripped off, told off, or pointed at in the street by strange men in green paper hats. So – *Go for it!*

HOW THIS BOOK WORKS

It couldn't be simpler. The book has been arranged in alphabetical order. So all you need is as basic an understanding of the alphabet, as I have, and you'll be able to use it. The information is arranged in subject headings. Sometimes these are very specific, as in: *Starting Your Own Unisex Hairdressing Business* (under "U" for "Unisex"), and sometimes they're very general, as in *Zits* (under "Z" for "Zits", surprisingly enough). All you need to do is work out exactly what you want to ask the book, and look it up. If you don't find the answer the first time, the book may well direct you to a different heading (as in: **SEE ALSO: HOSPITAL FOOD**). If you don't find the answer this time, the chances are that it's not in the book at all. But I can't think of everything, can I? I've tried to cover as wide a range of subjects as I can, and still allow you to fit the book in your pocket. For this is a book to carry about, a book to be seen with, a book to take with you wherever you go, especially the toilet. Incidentally, there is little or no information about toilet behaviour. I figured that if you'd got this far in life, you probably knew as much about it as I did. Anyway, I hope you enjoy the book, and that it improves the quality of your life (or makes you laugh, whichever's quicker).

A

ABSENCE *(Ab-sense):* If you are away from school, you tend to get marked as *Absent*, which basically means that you're not all there. Too much *Absence* can be a bad thing. Not because you'll miss learning something, but because you might get yourself involved in the awful pantomime of Bringing a Note. (**SEE ALSO: GETTING OUT OF GAMES, AVOIDING SHOWERS**).

Obviously a verbal excuse is acceptable if you haven't taken too much time off. For instance, if you've only taken a couple of days off, most teachers will accept the excuse that you were waiting for a bus. (In some areas this excuse holds good for a week. But be careful, because when the bus does come, it comes accompanied by so many other buses that the Waiting For A Bus excuse can't be used again for weeks.)

On the other hand, if you're away for several months, most teachers will assume that you've been lost on a cross-country run, and send flowers home to your parents (they might even have a collection).

But if you're only off for a few weeks, then the Note will be the only acceptable excuse. Otherwise most teachers get pretty cross, which is stupid, because there is an expression: "Absence makes the heart grow fonder." So, you'd think that the way to make yourself really popular with the teachers would be to stay away completely, wouldn't you? (**SEE ALSO: TEACHERS, SCHOOL: AVOIDING**)

ACAPELLA - WHAT IS IT? *(A-Cap-ELLa-Wotizzit?):* Basically it's a really cheap way of putting a band together, because no one needs an instrument! Imagine it: no arguments about who gets to do the showy guitar riff in the middle eight, no outrageous Hire Purchase repayments, no boring music lessons, and no heavy instruments to lug around. You could go on tour on the bus! All you need to be able to do is sing. No problem! Someone once said: "Everyone can sing", so that's what you tell the audience when they start shouting out that you can't. The audience might even throw fruit at you, which will save on the cost of tour caterers. A point here: if the audience insists on throwing avocados (this may happen in the posher parts of the country) try and persuade them to throw prawns, vinegar and mayonnaise as well, otherwise the avocados taste awful! (SEE ALSO: HIRE PURCHASE, LEARNING AN INSTRUMENT, TOURING WITH YOUR BAND/GROUP, FORMING A BAND, AVOCADO PEAR)

ACCOUNTANT: JOB OPPORTUNITY *(A-count-Ant: gob Opper-Tune-Itty):* A great (and highly paid) job for anyone who is good at Sums, or who owns a nice suit and looks as if they are good at Sums. Of course, this is not essential. For tax accountancy, for instance, a lack of knowledge of basic arithmetic is a definite advantage, as long as this is replaced by the ability to make figures look totally confusing. This is called Creative Accountancy. What is essential for any budding accountant is the ability to understand and handle a pocket calculator. For instance, did you know that if you punch Decimal point, 0,7,7,3,4 into a calculator, and then turn it upside down, it reads HELLO? If you didn't, then you'll never make an accountant, because this is the sort of stuff they do all the time. (SEE ALSO: POCKET CALCULATOR, HIGH COURT JUDGE, BARRISTER)

ACID HOUSE PARTIES: WHAT ARE THEY? *(A-Sid Howspa-Tiz: Wot-arthay?):* Of course, it is quite possible that by the time you read this, Acid House Parties will be a thing of the past. So maybe this entry should be called: "Acid House Parties: What *Were* They?". But currently they are huge Discos, attended by huge numbers of Young People, usually held in huge barns, aircraft hangars, etc. The accent is very much on *Huge*. Obviously, such an event attracts the atten-

tion of drug pushers and all other forms of Rip-off merchant: Acid House T-shirt Salesmen, Acid House Mug Salesmen, Acid House Badge Salesmen, Acid House Nodding Dog Salesmen and so on. Most of the Young People are wise and say "No, thank you very much, nice Mister Drug Pusher", and go on enjoying the party. Other less bright kids say "Yes, please, and can I have a mug as well?", and possibly don't live long enough to regret it.

Now, these Acid House Parties obviously also attract the attention of the Establishment, that group of self-appointed moral guardians who are opposed totally to the idea of large groups of Young People gathering together in one place (and yet they like schools. I don't understand that!). The upshot of this is that the police, who would far rather be indoors watching *The Bill*, have to turn up and put a stop to the party, get accused of being party-poopers, and don't even get offered a sausage roll. It all seems a bit of a pity, as long as the event is properly organized, doesn't break any laws, or annoy the neighbours. Oh, and as long as somebody vacuums round afterwards! (**SEE ALSO: DISCO, YOUR OWN DISCO: RUNNING, DRINK AND DRUGS, POLICE**)

ACNE *(Ac-knee):* (**SEE ZITS**) Also see under your armpits. If you've got spots under there, it may not be Acne at all. It might be Bubonic Plague, which is a far more long-term condition. In fact it's a condition that can't really be relieved at all, not even by singing "Ring-o-ring-o-roses". (**SEE ALSO: PLUKES, HOSPITAL FOOD**)

ACTS OF GOD - WHAT ARE THEY? *(Ax-of-GOD: Wotarthay?):* In the beginning God made Heaven and Earth. He made the Creatures of the Earth, the Beasts of the Field, the Fish of the Sea, and the Birds of the Air. He made Man in his own image, although this has been disputed many times since. Not surprisingly, really, because, for one thing, God probably didn't know what He looked like, as He had not yet made the Mirrors of the Bathroom, or indeed the Noodle of the Pot, the Instant Mash of the Potato, or the Contra-flow System of the Motorway (actually God never did make these things. By the time they came along, Man had taken over running things). Yes, I suppose God could have looked at his reflection in a river, but you have to remember that He made everything in six days, so I doubt very much that He had any time to play with His creations. But, anyway, He made Man. He called the Man Adam. You see, God knew that Man would get a hell of a lot of stick at school if He called him Tarquin. He then took a rib from Adam's body and made

8

Woman. (Adam would rather have had a pair of football boots, but God (being all-knowing, etc.) realized that playing football would only lead to a great wailing and gnashing of teeth, not to mention getting banned from Europe by UEFA.)

Now, we know that God did all this, because It is Writ, as they say in the Bible. Also, He told us. Nowadays things are different. People have stopped writing Bibles, and God

God making man: an early attempt

keeps a low profile. And what happens? He gets the blame for any unpleasant thing that happens: that gale a couple of years ago is a good example. The fact that the weather men all told us that it wasn't going to happen gets completely ignored. God takes the rap. Then there's British Rail. When a train is late, the announcement declares: "This is due to an Act of God."

I wonder what God thinks of the Channel Tunnel. Not a lot, I imagine. If He gave interviews, He'd probably say: "Listen. If I'd wanted England to be joined to France, I wouldn't have spent three-quarters of an hour putting 26 miles of water between them, would I?"

But God doesn't give interviews. God, like Royalty, doesn't answer back. Which means that, just like Royalty, He cops the blame for everything. (**SEE ALSO: QUEEN, GODS, JEHOVAH'S WITNESSES**)

ADOLESCENCE *(ADDle-ESSence):* This is an extract from

the tree of knowledge, that is traditionally fed to young people between childhood and adulthood, to make them feel totally confused. It usually causes no lasting harm, although no proper research has been done into this particular aspect.

ANORAXIA: CONDITION *(Anne-Or-Axia: Con-Dish-un):* Anoraxia is not fatal, but you rarely grow out of it. In simple lay person's terms, it manifests itself in the wearing of quilted nylon coats. It tends to afflict you more readily if you're called Colin, or if you Collect Stamps, Spot Trains (unless you're a pigeon), or play Dungeons and Dragons. Although it isn't contagious, sufferers do tend to keep themselves pretty well to themselves, and they can often be seen in small pathetic groups, hanging around outside Army Surplus Stores, Book Fairs and Beer Festivals. Some of them can be surprisingly intelligent, a fact that you would never glean from their appearance. Anoraxia can also affect your eyesight, and sufferers often wear glasses. They also keep a sticking plaster handy (usually on the side of their glasses) in case they cut themselves. (**SEE ALSO: STAMP COLLECTING, TRAIN SPOTTING, FOLK MUSIC**)

AUSTRALIAN *(Orst-raily-'n):* It's amazing how much you can learn about a country, its people, and their culture, just by watching Television. Which is quite handy really, because that's all a lot of people ever do. Take Australia, for example: simply by watching Australian soap operas, I have learned all of the following. The Australian male is incapable of coherent speech unless he has a can of lager in his hand. Dinner guests are always entertained in the back garden and fed burnt food – this is called a Barbi. Oh, and all Australian doctors fly about in aeroplanes. Which must make it very difficult to make house-calls in built-up areas! Just getting permission to land would be a major operation.

Now, this is probably very unfair. After all, I'd hate to think what Australians think of us, after watching *Eastenders*, and

Never The Twain! They hardly reflect English life as we know it. However, if Australian TV is in any way accurate, then I've also picked up some useful Australian words (and there was me thinking that they spoke English!):

Arvo: Which means *Afternoon*, as in "I'll see you this Arvo." ("I'll see you this afternoon.")

Deck: Means to flatten someone, put them on the deck. It probably dates back to when the first Australian settlers went out there on the boats, or Convict Ships, as they were called then. Any argument, and there were probably hundreds if *Home and Away* is anything to go by, would undoubtedly result in one or all of the participants ending up On The Deck, having been offered the traditional British Bunch Of Fives. (**SEE ALSO: BUNCH OF FIVES**)

An Australian map of the world

G'day: means good day, which in Australia is a greeting, whereas in this country it is something we say when we leave. This is obviously one of the major cultural differences.

Rage: Means a party or a good time. Thus "We're really raging!" means "We're really having a good time." *Raging* in English means "Going completely berserk". Maybe it does in Australia, too. After all, I've never been to an Australian party . . .

Sheila: This is what all Australian women are actually called, although for the sake of TV soap operas, they're given different names, like Madge and Charlene. If they didn't, it would get awfully confusing, wouldn't it? I mean more confusing than it actually is. Gosh! You might have to concentrate in order to follow the plot, which would rather defeat the whole object of soaps.

Tinnies: This is Australian for lager, because all their beer comes in tins. From the taste I imagine it's probably brewed that way. They also say "Crack a tube", when they mean "Have a drink". This is a reference to the quaint Australian custom of hitting each other over the head with empty beer cans. (**SEE ALSO: KYLIE MINOGUE'S HAIRDRESSER, JASON DONOVAN**)

AUTOBIOGRAPHY: DEFINITION *(ORto-biOG-raffy: Deaf-inISHen):* A book about a famous personality, written by their car. (**SEE ALSO: BIOGRAPHY**)

AVOCADO *('Ave-a Cardo):* A colour, which basically comes in two forms: pears and bathroom suites. The trick is not to confuse the two. The easiest way to avoid this confusion is to remember this simple rule: avocado pears often tend to be full of prawns, whereas avocado bathroom suites often tend to be full of water, and naked bodies, but not prawns. This is, of course, not always the case. There are probably many instances of people filling their bath with prawns, although I think it's unlikely you'll find an avocado pear full of naked bodies (unless the definition of *naked* extends to prawns with

Pear   Bathroom suite

their shells off). If you are in any doubt, I suggest you avoid bathing and eating out (**SEE ALSO: AVOCADO PEAR, EATING OUT**)

AVOCADO PEAR – WHAT IS IT? *('Ave-a-Cardo-pair: WotIZZit?):* When seen in shops – usually fruit shops (although some of the better supermarkets may stock them) – avocados can look unprepossessing. Not to mention horrible. They look rather like large green prunes. Having located what you believe may be an avocado, pick it up and press it gently, but firmly, between the thumb and forefinger of your right hand. If it is hard, then it is not ripe and you shouldn't buy it. If, on the other hand, a nasty green slime spurts out of it, then the pear is over-ripe, and you shouldn't buy it, either. An avocado pear has to be "just right". If in doubt, ask the stall-holder. He will, more than likely, throw the pear a casual glance (this is the Expert's body language for "I don't know") and say: "It's just right." You will be none the wiser, and will

13

probably buy it anyway. Once you have got it home, which will not be difficult as it is only the size of a piece of fruit, you will need to halve it and remove the stone, which surprisingly enough you will find in the middle of the pear. You are then left with the Flesh – the bit you eat. This, you will notice, is a sort of sickly green colour. (The same green as they use to paint hospital walls. In fact it has the same *texture* as the green paint they use for hospital walls. It probably has the same taste too. I wouldn't know, I've never actually eaten hospital paint. But if hospital food is anything to go by, it must be pretty revolting.) (**SEE ALSO: HOSPITAL FOOD, EATING OUT**)

AVOIDING SHOWERS *(A-voi-Ding Shou-erz):* If your forged note has succeeded in getting you out of games (**SEE ALSO: GETTING OUT OF GAMES**), the chances are that it will help you avoid having a shower too. If, however, this is not the case, then a separate Shower Note might have to be on stand-by. (In fact, it's always quite a good idea to have a selection of notes available at all times).

So, what should the Shower Note say? Well, I think you'll find that the good old *Verruca* still weaves the same magic spell over health-conscious Sports Teachers that it always has. For those of you who've never come across a Verruca (not a very sensible thing to do) it is a wart, sometimes found on the foot, but usually only found in forged notes. It has the reputation of being lethal at twenty paces, although it is almost impossible to infect another person without actually rubbing your feet together with theirs. Now, I don't know what you get up to in PE, but when I was a lad such intimacy was usually saved for behind-the-bike-sheds, and even then we never got as far as rubbing feet (incidentally, you cannot get pregnant by rubbing feet, as long as you are wearing safe socks). (**SEE ALSO: SCHOOL: POINT OF, SCHOOL: AVOIDING, TEACHERS**)

B

BAD BREATH: FACT AND FABLE *(Badbreth: Facten-fabul):* Bad breath, in common with Body Odour, has a very negative profile, as they probably say in advertising. All that basically means is that people would rather not have it. They'd rather have a 24-speed mountain bike than bad breath. In fact, they'd probably rather have a Des O'Connor album than bad breath. Some people may even rather be a member of *Rolf Harris's Cartoon Club* than have bad breath, although that might be an over-statement. But is Bad Breath really that awful? It is a question of degree, although you don't need to have a degree to catch it. But it really isn't such a terrible thing to have. Unless you want to kiss someone, speak, open your mouth or breathe . . .

But Bad Breath is controllable. It is often caused by what you eat. They say You Are What You Eat, and in the case of your breath, this is very true. So, avoiding the kind of foods that make your breath smell is the first step. This includes spicy foods, garlic, dog biscuits, or anything you see lying in the road that you cannot immediately identify. (**SEE ALSO: KEEPING PETS**) "But I love curry," I hear you whinge. So do I, and there's no reason why you shouldn't go on enjoying it. The trick is to make sure that whoever you're with eats the same meal. So, next time you bring a Take-Away Elk Vindaloo into the Common Room, make sure you bring enough for everyone.

Testing for Bad Breath:
There is a simple test you can carry out if you are worried that you may have bad breath. Place your hand a few inches from your mouth, breathe on your hand, and then quickly sniff. However, the test is not very reliable, because the smell that comes back to you usually depends on where you've had your hand recently. And if you wash your hand prior to the test, the only thing you are likely to smell is cheap soap. (**SEE ALSO: SOAP**) If, however your entire hand withers and drops off, you can take it as fairly likely that you've got bad breath.
NOTE: Bad Breath is not to be confused with Brandreth, which is a totally different complaint, difficult to detect and almost impossible to treat. (**SEE ALSO: BODY ODOUR, BRANDRETH, YOU ARE WHAT YOU EAT**)

BARRISTER: JOB OPPORTUNITY *(Barry-Ster: Gob-Opper Tune-Itty):* Another great job for anyone who likes dressing up and wearing a wig, but hasn't quite got the courage to go the whole hog. Barristers tend to wear proper trousers, unlike High Court Judges, who wear a form of Panty Hose. (**SEE ALSO: HIGH COURT JUDGE**) They are also known to wear skirts, although there are too few female Barristers. The other major difference is that they wear a smaller wig, more like a toupee. Many popular entertainers, such as Bruce Forsyth and Frankie Howerd, could be Barristers. They may even have considered the career, although discovering that being Called To The Bar had nothing to do with going to the Pub might have put them off. Unlike a High Court Judge, a Barrister does need a qualification. They need to be able to argue without resorting to the Bunch of Fives. (**SEE: BUNCH OF FIVES**) Oh, and they also need a plummy voice. (**SEE ALSO: BRANDRETH**) A vague knowledge of the Law and enough Latin to baffle the jury would help. Facial tattoos and nostril rings wouldn't. (**SEE ALSO: ACCOUNTANT**)

BEAUTY WITHOUT CRUELTY: WHAT IS IT? *(Byoo-tee-withote-crewl-tea: Wotizzit?):* Nowadays, there is growing concern about the rights of animals: whether they should be turned into coats, have shampoo squirted in their eyes, or even be eaten. Naturally, animals have no say in this. Were we able to ask them whether they wanted to be dissected, taught to smoke etc., they would more than likely say "No thanks". So, since animals can't express their own opinions, other than by running away, we have to decide for them. And that's where the problem lies. You see, while most people would agree that it isn't necessary to squirt shampoo in the rabbit's eye in order to find out whether it stings – particularly as rabbits don't have tear-ducts in order to wash the shampoo out again, or a voice with which to say: "Ouch! That stings!" – a lot of people do like to eat a nice juicy steak, beefburgers, lamb and pork; in fact the list is endless.

So, where do you draw the line? Certainly turning an animal into a pot roast is a lot less painful for it than experimenting on it, as long as you kill it first. But it is still a dilemma. What can we do? One answer might be only to experiment on those animals we intend to eat. For instance, herrings could be used for smoking experiments, and then they'd already be kippered. Also we could wear the skins and coats of the animals we experiment on or eat. The big fashion houses could start a trend for chicken feather coats. Bring back Kipper Ties! It may not be much, but it's a start! (SEE ALSO: VEGGIES)

BIOGRAPHY *(Bye-OG-raffy):* A book written about a person. This person is usually famous or infamous, although they don't have to be. They can become famous for having books written about them. But usually they are personalities: Film Stars, Inventors, Discoverers, TV Stars, Mass Murderers, etc. There are often several versions of the same book. Or, at least, several books written about the same person. Therefore you get the *Unofficial* Biography, which is usually the Truth, and the *Official* Biography, which tends to be the version which the famous person wants people to believe. Sometimes the Famous Person will help write the book, which means that it often gets even further from the Truth. Sometimes the Famous Person will actually write it themselves, or have it *Ghost Written*. No, this doesn't mean that they get it written by a ghost or a dead person, although very often it reads as if it has been. It means that they get a proper writer

IT WAS AT THE AGE OF TWO AND A HALF WHEN I KNEW THE STAGE WOULD BE MY LIFE!

to do the writing, correct the spelling, check for libel, etc. In this instance the book cover often says *As Told To . . .*

The reason that Famous People have their biographies written while they are still alive is usually due to one thing – money . . . or a lack of it. You may be watching *Wogan* one night, and some Famous Person comes on and starts talking about a book that has been written about them. Almost certainly someone in your living room will suddenly say, "Cor! I haven't seen that Famous Person for years!", which explains the book. They need the money. You see, a lot of Famous People will do anything to make money, even go on *Wogan*!

BODY ODOUR *(Bo-Dee O-Der):* Body odour is a difficult thing to handle, because it's one of those things that you never really know you've got. Oh, yes, you can tell if your armpit is a bit whiffy simply by sticking your nose in it. Not a thing, incidentally, to do in polite company, or in front of your date. (**SEE ALSO: IMPRESSING YOUR DATE**) But real 24-Carat Body Pong, that's a different matter. It's strange, isn't it, that someone else's pong is really obvious, and yet it's hard to detect your own. It is a source of worry for many people. Some blokes, of course, are probably under the delusion that the fact that girls faint when they walk into the room is due to their animal magnetism, not the fact that they smell like the floor of the elephant house in Regent's Park Zoo.

So, how do you find out if you whiff? Relying on the reactions of people when you enter a room can be misleading. The fact that they screw their faces up on seeing you could be due to the fact that you're ugly, not smelly. Asking someone is one way. But be careful who you ask. You need to be sure that they have your best interests at heart. A parent is a good choice, although don't pick a bad time. If you interrupt some really important parental duty, such as watching a Video Nasty to make sure it's suitable for your six-year-old brother's birthday party, you are likely to get a "Yes! Now clear off!", whether you do or not. Asking your date can also be a mistake. Particularly if you're snuggled up on the back row at the pictures. And, more especially if the answer is: "Well, yes. You do, actually". It can put a damper on the whole evening. Of course, your date may try to let you know, with subtle, almost undetectable, signals and signs, such as wearing a gas mask.

I suppose the answer to body odour is to be careful about your personal hygiene. Bath or shower regularly. Wash your clothes at least once a year. Avoid sleeping in the same straw as your rabbits (it's not your fault that they're afraid of the dark). But, above all, don't worry unnecessarily. If your date doesn't mind cuddling up to you, the chances are that you don't smell. Unless, of course, they suffer from sinus trouble. Or unless they smell as well! (**SEE ALSO: BAD BREATH**)

BONNIE LANGFORD: CONDITION *(Bonny Lang-Fudd: Con Dishun):* The feeling that you are Shirley Temple, but waking up eventually to the fact that you are not. Unfortunately, the cute image projected during the sufferer's Shirley Temple phase is very hard to get rid of. However, one bonus of this condition is the ability to frighten dogs by just one line from a popular song. This even works on Rottweilers. (**SEE ALSO: ROTTWEILERS**)

BOUNCE: DEFINITION *(Bouns: Deaf-in-ISHan):* Bounce is an essential quality for the young TV Presenter, particularly on Children's TV. And even more particularly if they want to appear Wacky and Zany. Bounce is also a dog food. Whether would-be young TV Presenters have to eat the dog food in order to get the quality, I have so far failed to find out. Certainly, some young TV Presenters are thin enough to suggest that they live on a diet of dog food. (**SEE ALSO: TV PRESENTER (CHILDREN'S), WACKY, ZANY**)

BRACES: *(Bray-sez):* There comes a time, usually at the very moment that you start fancying the opposite sex, that your parents decide that your teeth are crooked, and immediately get a dentist to slap a huge great metal brace on your teeth. The result of this is that you are afraid to smile (or go near a magnet). Naturally this kills any possibility of your getting off with the person of your dreams, which is probably why your parents did it in the first place! I mean, even if you *look* fine, you *feel* like a freak. And it's no consolation to know that this freaky feeling is all in your head, because that's where the brace is too! What's worse, if the love of your life also has a brace there's no way you can kiss without getting locked together. This is of course quite pleasant for the first ten minutes, but can become a drag very quickly, especially if you like breathing. Incidentially, don't confuse teeth braces with the type of braces you use to hold your jeans up, or you could really be in trouble. You'll have to unzip your fly in order to speak, and won't be able to pull your jeans on without biting yourself in the bum.

A bad attack of Brandreth

BRANDRETH: WHAT IS IT? *(Brain-death: Wotizzit?):* An unpleasant condition, causing a feeling of nausea in the morning, between six and nine-thirty. Here its similarity to pregnancy ends, since pregnancy has a happy end result, whereas Brandreth offers no such hope. Exposure to this condition is more or less harmless in very small doses. In fact, it is only *bearable* in very small doses. Symptoms are: burbling in an inane, plumby-voiced manner, the wearing of ludicrous home-knitted sweaters all year round, and the reading aloud of letters (written by people suffering from the same condition), which contain such gems as: "My gerbil sings the Russian national anthem", "Why does nobody stay for the credits at the end of films?" (in case they play the national anthem, that's why) and "Hanging's too good for them!" If left untreated, this condition can develop into full-blown Rantzen, which, as you probably know, is totally incurable. However, if Brandreth is caught (and locked up) early enough, you may suffer no lasting side-effects (except perhaps the odd knitted tie). **(SEE ALSO: RANTZEN, GAME SHOWS)**

BUILT-IN OBSOLESCENCE: *(Bill-tin Ob-sol-S-Hans):* "Nothing lasts for ever," some wise old person once said. Probably just before they died, thus not actually being there to witness the wisdom of their words, or say "I told you so". But what is Built-In Obsolescence? It's that little something that the manufacturers add to their product to ensure that you buy another one. "I thought that was called *quality*?" I hear you say. No! Far from it! You see, the reason you want another one is not because the last one was so amazing, but because the last one fell to bits. This explains why the wheel fell off your tricycle when you were little, nine months before you had outgrown it, forcing your parents to buy you a new one, which you outgrew and which then got stuffed in the shed until your baby brother was large enough to use it. And what happened then? Two hours and thirty-two seconds after your little brother first mounted the trike, the wheel fell off! Amazing! Have you any idea how much money is spent on research to ensure that the wheel falls off just at the right moment so that no one actually gets hurt, but someone gets lumbered with buying a new one? Billions of pounds. But much less than the profits from the sales of the new ones.

Then there are light bulbs. On the face of it, a light bulb should last for years, as long as it is used properly, and not hit with hammers, stood on, or pushed up a nostril. So why don't they? Simple, the light bulb works on the principle of an electric charge being passed through a vacuum. If you introduce the minutest amount of air into this vacuum, the light bulb will stop working. This usually happens late at night, when you are standing at the top of a wobbly stepladder on the landing, getting your old Action Man/Sindy Doll out of the attic so that you can check that they still haven't got any naughty bits. (**SEE ALSO: HOSPITAL FOOD**)

But it doesn't stop at light bulbs. Oh no! This same technology is behind the fact that the arm falls off Crud the Enforcer on the very day that its creators, Heroes of Death

Toys Inc., launch their latest model, Conan the Librarian. Other items well known for their built-in obsolescence include cars, stereo systems ("Sorry, we just can't get the parts.") and computers. Diamonds, though, are for ever. But that's only because no one has yet devised a way of making them fall apart!

BUNCH OF FIVES: DEFINITION *(Bunsherfives: Deaf-in-Ishen):* There will be times in your life when you find yourself in the middle of an argument, and you are offered a Bunch of Fives. You may think that you are having a *discussion*, but if it has reached this point, then take my word for it – it is probably an *argument*. So what exactly is a Bunch of Fives? Well, in simple lay-person's terms, it is an alternative way of winning

an argument. Assume that you are in the middle of a discussion, and things are going your way. It is quite likely that your opponent will suddenly say, "Do you want a Bunch of Fives?" Hopefully you will have looked up the definition before you reach this point, because you won't be given the opportunity to look it up there and then. Your best answer would be, "No, thank you", although they may still give you the Bunch of Fives anyway. If this happens, your best course of action is to take the Bunch of Fives straight indoors and run it under the tap. Your opponent may, of course, offer you a Fourpenny One instead. This sounds less than a Bunch of Fives, but it might not be. (SEE ALSO: HOSPITAL FOOD, SELF DEFENCE)

BUYING A MUSICAL INSTRUMENT *(By-ing amuse-Iccle Ins-Trumm-Unt):* Elsewhere in this book I have discussed Forming A Band, and obviously at some point that band will need to buy instruments. This can be very tricky indeed. Naturally, just finding something to hold on *Top of the Pops* is not too difficult. If the worst comes to the worst, the BBC props department has a good selection of dummy instruments that you could borrow. But if your band is going on tour, or even playing in public (not necessarily the same thing), then you will need your own instrument. The BBC will not take kindly to your taking theirs home with you.

But before you take a trip to the local music store, ask around the family. There was a time when every family had at least one person who was musical. Often they could play the piano, sometimes only the spoons but it's worth asking. They may still have their instrument hidden away somewhere.

Failing this, take yourself off to the local music store. This is where the trouble starts. Picking an instrument isn't that difficult. Go for something with "Street Cred". Avoid cow bells and triangles. But be careful. Before you select your instrument, remember that you are going to be under a certain amount of pressure to learn to play it, particularly if your parents have helped you pay for it. So choose something that isn't too complex, doesn't have too many sticking-out twiddly bits on it. Oh, and get something that is going to be easy to keep clean. Remember the hassle you have with your bike! A lot of music shops are run by musicians, so you'll find them quite helpful, if you can hold their attention long enough to ask for help. (**SEE ALSO: MUSO**)

Most music shops will let you play the instruments. If in doubt, ask an assistant. Or look for little tell-tale signs, such as a notice on the wall reading: "Anyone touching the instruments will get their head nailed to the floor." Don't pick an instrument up without asking. This can save you a lot of hassle. Particularly in the case of a grand piano. If you ask first, the assistant will point out that you're not strong enough to pick up the grand piano, and, anyway, it isn't played under the chin. (**SEE ALSO: LEARNING AN INSTRUMENT**) If you take a mate with you, select one who knows even less about musical instruments than you do. A member of your band would be a good choice.

Having bought your instrument you may need a few accessories. Allow for the cost of this when you are budgeting. An electric guitar, for instance, will also need an amplifier. A small one will do to start with, just for practising (if you intend to practise, that is). You may also need a lead, but only if you are thinking of connecting the guitar to the amp. This is only necessary if you intend to play Live (you won't need a lead to appear on TV, for instance). Which brings me to another point: if your band intends to tour, pick an instrument that is easy to pack away. The drummer is always left unscrewing his hi-hat while the rest of the band are in the Chinese restaurant (so if you don't like Chinese food, be a drummer!). A final word of warning, don't let your little brother or sister fiddle with it. It can be really humiliating if a five-year-old gets a recognizable tune out of it before you do! Another final word of warning: whatever instrument you buy, don't forget to get a plug! (**SEE ALSO: WHY DO YOU NEVER GET A PLUG?**)

C

CHANNEL FOUR *(Channel 4):* This is the TV channel that nobody watches. Or at least it *was*, until they introduced Sky Television. (**SEE ALSO: MAKING YOUR OWN SATELLITE DISH**)

CHRIS QUINTEN: CONDITION: *(Kris-Quin-Tin: Con Dishon):* This tends to afflict actors more than any others. It is a state brought on by too much exercise, which looks very much like *Rigor Mortis*. Although the person is still walking and talking, after a fashion, he appears to be as stiff as a corpse. Edward Woodward (aptly named) is showing the early symptoms in *The Equaliser*. It doesn't actually prevent the actor from working, and can develop so well that the actor finds himself married to a millionaire American TV presenter. (**SEE ALSO: FAME, POSERS, POP FAME**)

COIN COLLECTING: HOBBY *(Coyne-colleck-Tin: Hobbee):* This is one of the simplest hobbies to get into. All you require to start it off are a few coins. These can be found in various places around the home: pockets, old jam jars, tins labelled "Milk Money", "Rent", that sort of thing. In no time at all you could have quite a decent collection. Naturally you may have a few duplicates, which really won't be a lot of use to your collection. I suggest that

Coin collecting can be a lifetime hobby

27

you send them to my Swiss bank account, and I'll put them to very good use. (**SEE ALSO: HOBBIES**)

COLLECTABLES: WHO NEEDS THEM? *(Col-Eck-tubbles: Hoo-Neadz-Thum?):* Well, we all do, apparently. At least, that's what the advertisers tell us. It's all very clever, really. So, what are they, these Collectables? Well, they can range from plastic figures with moving bits (not to mention bits that drop off) (**SEE ALSO: BUILT-IN OBSOLESCENCE**), via "cute" little ponies, right through to very expensive hand-crafted china ornaments. But they all have one thing in common. They are hyped up to the sky, so that the buyers simply *must* have every one of them. Oh, and the other thing they all have in common is the fact that they are very expensive, not to mention tacky. (**SEE ALSO: RIP-OFFS**)

So, why do we buy them? Well, in the case of collectables aimed at children, they tend to be linked to a cartoon series. It's often difficult to work out which came first, the collectable or the series. I can tell you the answer to that: they are born together at the same meeting, called specifically to discuss ways of making a lot of money. But the effect of the cartoon series is to make you want to own the figure, so that you can live out the fantasy events portrayed in the series. And the effect of the figure is to make you want to watch the series. And the collective effect of the figures and the series is to make you need more pocket money. Clever, eh? (**SEE ALSO: STAMP COLLECTING, COIN COLLECTING, TRAIN SPOTTING, ANORAXIA, HOBBIES**)

COMPETITION *(Comper-TISHon):* There was a time, not too long ago, when someone, in their wisdom, decided that Competition was "a bad thing", and that we should do away with competitive sport in schools, because it encouraged people to compete against each other. I think this decision was made on a Thursday. By the Friday the decision had been reversed, and it was decided that competitive sport was, after all, a "good thing". This is the sort of about-turn that Educationalists make all the time. It's what we pay them for. Still, it keeps them off the streets, not to mention getting them excused from competitive sport without having to bring a note. (**SEE: GETTING OUT OF GAMES**)

But what is a non-competitive race? Presumably it's one where all the runners attempt to come second equal. After all, if they win, it means someone else has lost. And if they lose, it means that someone else has won. It is like football without goal-posts, just a lot of running about, trying to avoid the ball. Mind you, when I was at school, I thought that's how football was played. And if I'm completely honest, I haven't really seen much evidence to suggest that it isn't in this country. (**SEE ALSO: FOOTBALL**)

Anyway, is competition really such a bad thing? Our lives are full of it. Throughout our time at school, we are continually put in positions where we compete with our classmates, from the simplest spelling test, to the school sports day. The only way to remove competitiveness from, say, a spelling test would be not to tell any of the pupils how many spellings they got right, so that they wouldn't be able to compare their results with anyone elses. But in order to do this, the teacher would not be able to tell you *which* spellings you got right, and that would defeat the object of the test! (**SEE ALSO: FOOTBALL, CRICKET, WIMBLEDON**)

CONTACT LENSES *(Con-Tact Len Ziz):* One of the greatest frustrations of the twentieth century, or maybe two of the greatest frustrations, are contact lenses. Yes, I know that glasses fall off when you're jogging, steam up in the bath, and drop in your yoghurt, but at least they don't fall out, causing everyone in a twenty-mile radius to become a gibbering wreck! So why do people wear contact lenses? Vanity. They don't want other people to know that they're short-sighted. As if anyone else cares! They care far more if they're made to crawl around for hours, patting the carpet! Being in the theatre I have had a good deal of first-hand experience of both vanity and contact lenses. Imagine the scene (Scene 3, Act 5 of Shakespeare's little known Comi-Tragedy *Trevor Of Lytham St. Annes*): The King of All the Jutes has just put all his relatives (those, that is, whose names begin with a W) to the sword for forgetting his birthday. Enter Simeon The Untidy:

> **SIMEON**: My Lord, Bess The Flatulent is without.
> **TREVOR**: Bid her enter.
> TRUMPETS, HORNS, AND OTHER STRANGE NOISES OFF. ENTER BESS THE FLATULENT WITH FULL ENTOURAGE, INCLUDING THE KEEPER OF THE ROYAL ANDREWS.
> **BESS**: Greetings from the distant . . . (SUDDENLY THROWS UP ARMS IN ALARM) Argh! Don't anybody move!

At this point the audience, being unfamiliar with this play (it's never been on television), assumes that Bess is staging some form of medieval military coup. Not at all. Rosamund Sax-Hylton, the actress currently bringing an entirely original interpretation to the part of Bess, has lost a contact lens. The uppermost thought in her mind right now is not the suspension of the audience's disbelief, but the fact that they cost her £170. They're lightly tinted, which is actually going to make them even harder to find, as they blend perfectly with the stage-cloth. The entire cast, including the Dukes of Ingle and of Strooth, down swords, and start crawling around patting the stage, and muttering "Where did you drop it?" How stupid! If she knew *that* it wouldn't be lost, would it?

Only the actor playing the lead makes any attempt to confuse the audience into thinking that this is part of the show (he was once in *Howard's Way* and has a reputation to rebuild). He chants in a high falsetto, thus turning the whole thing into some strange pagan ceremony. After twenty minutes, even he abandons any attempt at deception, and soon the entire audience are on their hands and knees. The theatre critic of the *Evening Post*, arriving late (he got held up in the bar), misinterprets the audience's reaction as mass adulation, and his revue the next day makes the show an overnight success. The contact lens, however, is gone. It has been crushed underfoot by Denzil the Semi-retired, played (with great effort) by an actor who is himself very short-sighted, but refuses to make any concession to the fact, other than the carrying of a silver-knobbed white stick. All in all, I think I'll stick to glasses. (**SEE ALSO: OPTICIAN, RIP-OFFS**)

CREDIT: WHAT IS IT? *(Cred It: Wotizzit?):* There will be times when you want to buy something, but can't afford it. At times like this you will be offered Credit. So what *is* it, exactly? Well, if you look up the definition of Credit in a dictionary, you'll be very encouraged to discover that it means things like: Confidence, Faith, Trust, Honour, Merit and Praise. You will be less encouraged to discover, when you go to buy something on it, that Credit is really badly named! Credit is the new modern term for Hire Purchase. (**SEE: HIRE PURCHASE**)

CRICKET: WHAT'S IT ALL ABOUT? *(Crikitt: Wotsit-or-labowt):* At first sight, Cricket would appear to be just a game – a gentle slow, almost stationary game. At least, that's the way the England team play it, anyway. It was first played in the 1300s, and has been played, after a fashion, ever since. So, why has the sport lasted such a long time, given that the English must have realized some time ago that they weren't any good at it? Well, the reason why Cricket is still being played can be traced back to the invention of Television by John Logie Baird, in 1926.

THERE'S CRICKET ON THE TELLY AGAIN....

When TV first appeared on the scene (and on the screen), it was seen as A Good Thing, giving endless opportunities to show old war films and things with Julie Andrews in them. But, as time went on, and everyone kept complaining about repeats, TV developed. Children's TV programmes started being made. Admittedly they weren't very good. Everyone in them spoke in strange, "posh", incomprehensible, plummy voices. (**SEE ALSO: BRANDRETH**) But at least children had something they could call their own. Then a younger breed of Children's TV programme makers came along: people who actually knew about the things that children liked. People who had in fact once been children themselves. This upset the Establishment, who believed that children should be Seen And Not Heard, certainly not heard enjoying themselves. Something had to be done. Children had to be encouraged to turn off the TV set. After all, it had already been established that most adults didn't know how to. And this is where Cricket came in. By replacing Children's TV programmes with Cricket from time to time, hundreds of children were soon switching off their sets. Of course, Cricket can't take all the credit. But following its success as a real turn-off, Snooker, Wimbledon, Party Political Conferences and *Young Doctors* soon followed. All with equal success.

Some bright spark, seeing how well the scheme had worked, suggested that the same system could be used to stop grown-ups watching TV. Unfortunately, the Snooker, Cricket, etc., were put on to adult TV very late at night, thus failing to prevent the viewing of the really dangerous TV programmes, such as *Never The Twain*, *That's My Dog*, and *Bob's Full House*. (**SEE ALSO: GAME SHOWS**)

D

DATES: HOW TO GET *(Daitz: How-2-gett):* We've all been there. There's this person at school/college/work, who we fancy so much that we keep eating our pencil. But what can we do about it? Of course there are always those flash people who no sooner start fancying someone than they start going out with them. What is it they've got that the rest of us haven't? Charisma? Charm? Money? Or do they just boast a lot? Assuming that you, like me and most other people, are not blessed with this special magic quality, what do you do? How do you get someone to go out with you? Wait until they fancy you? Tell them? Get your mate to tell them? (That can be dodgy, because your mate might wind up going out with them instead.) I suppose you could take out a full-page advert in the morning paper. Or hire an aeroplane to fly over their house, trailing one of those big signs, saying something like: "Tracy Skoggins (or Daryl Pencil), will you go out with me, please?" This is tricky on two counts. Firstly, they may not be called Tracy Skoggins (or even Daryl Pencil), and secondly, they may not be looking out of the window at the time that the plane flies over. But there are other, simpler and cheaper ways that are well within the reach of the average love-sick person. The techniques can vary from sex to sex, but the end result can often be the same. For example, if you're a **girl**:

(1) *Follow Him Everywhere*: Not very subtle, but it'll certainly get you noticed. There is a strong risk of him thinking that he's been put under surveillance by the KGB, though.

(2) *Draw Attention To Yourself*. This can be achieved by hitting him. But be careful, because unless you know your own strength, you might wind up doing him serious injury, in which case the only date you'll get will be visiting him in

hospital. Which means *you'll* wind up buying the grapes!
(**SEE ALSO: HOSPITAL FOOD**)

(3) *Send Messages To Him*: This can work, and is certainly
subtler than hitting him. Make sure, though, that he knows
the messages are from you. Make sure you're in the room
when he receives them, so that you can help with any long
words, joined-up writing, etc. This also ensures that your
mate doesn't try to get off with him. Your attitude while he
is reading your note should at all times be that of studied
indifference, as if it's nothing to do with you. Be careful
that you don't do this *too* well, though, or he might think
that the note is a forgery! (**SEE ALSO: JOINED-UP WRITING**)

(4) *Share His Interests*: This is really subtle, or at least it can

be if it's done properly. Make him aware of you by Being Around. (Don't confuse this with Being Round, which means getting so fat that he can't possibly miss you. (**SEE ALSO: FAT: AM I?, DIETING**)) If he plays football, stand around on the touchline, freezing to death (obviously stop this if it looks like becoming literally true). If he plays cricket, hang around the nets; if he hang-glides, let him spot you sitting casually up a tree, etc. But don't hang around the court if he plays squash – obviously! Now, showing an interest in *his* interests has the added bonus of helping you find out about him. You might discover just in time that he's a Closet Train-Spotter. It could mean the difference between getting lumbered and having a narrow escape.

(5) *Totally Ignore Him*: This is by far the subtlest way to get a guy to go out with you. The only trouble is, it is *so* subtle that he might not even realize you're doing it, unless of course you've already tried (1), (2), (3) and (4) with disastrous results. Though, if that's the case, he'll probably be extremely relieved that you're ignoring him.

It's no easier for **boys**:

Follow her or hit her, and you'll be in for it. Sending her notes could work, if you don't mind running the risk of having them read out loud in front of the entire class. Trying to share her interests might raise people's eyebrows quicker than it raises your hopes, particularly if she's into knitting. Yes, I know. There's no reason why a bloke shouldn't knit. But it still causes funny looks, I knitted a scarf once, and caused a great deal of winking and nudging. Mind you, I was knitting it at the Ballet!

You could become a Captain of Sport, win cups and win drawer-fulls of high jump medals, but make sure she's into sporty blokes before you work up a sweat. Not all girls are, you know!

* * *

36

Probably the simplest, most straightforward way for either sex to get a date with someone is to *ask* them. After all, what can they do? Call the police and have you arrested? Shoot you? Say no? Say Yes? There's a fifty-fifty chance of them saying yes. If they say no, don't make the mistake of saying "Why?" The chances are they'll tell you! This is of course one way of discovering things about yourself that you didn't know, but it isn't the best way. (**SEE: BODY ODOUR**)

So. Suppose you've asked someone out (having first checked that they're not armed), and they've said "Yes". Obviously you'll want to know why. *But don't ask*, in case they change their mind. But do try to find out if they have agreed to go out with you because:

    (A) They really like you.
    (B) They feel sorry for you.
    (C) They're doing it for a bet.

Let's hope that it's (A)! If it's (B) there's not much to be done, except make sure they pay. But if it's (C) then the best thing to do is agree to go out with them only if they split their winnings with you. (**SEE ALSO: IMPRESSING YOUR DATE, EATING OUT**)

DENTIST: JOB OPPORTUNITY *(Den-tist: Gob-Opper Tune-Itty):* If you've always had a thing about looking in people's mouths, and I'm not talking about just looking for lost chewing gum (**SEE ALSO: KISSING**), then Dentist could be the job for you. Obviously it requires a certain amount of skill, but not too much because you can always put your patients out while you operate. That way they won't see your mistakes. And once you've made a bit of money, you'll be able to employ another Dentist who knows what they're doing. There is in fact quite a killing (financial killing, that is!) to be made in dentistry. They get paid so much per tooth, which is why they fill rather than pull. (Talking of Pulling, dentistry is also a surprisingly romantic profession!) Dentistry a very good example of something that has changed out of all recognition over

the years. Some dentists have even installed TV in their surgeries! Have you ever tried watching TV when you're flat on your back with a mouthful of medical instruments? Actually, some programmes look better like that . . . (SEE ALSO: **MAKING YOUR OWN SATELLITE DISH**)

DIETING: THE THIN END OF THE WEDGE *(Die-ert-ing: the thinend-ovthe-weg):* The major reason that people diet is peer pressure. This peer pressure is usually inspired by media pressure. The media dictates that Thin is best, Tall is beautiful, etc. An individual becomes obsessed with losing weight, diets, becomes self-righteous about their self-sacrifice ("I've given up sugar *completely*!"), and therefore puts pressure upon others who are less weight-conscious. The net result is that the whole group become weight-conscious, and some of them wind up thoroughly miserable (or worse). The whole thing about weight and dieting is: are you happy with your own body, you great fat slug? If you are. Fine. If you're not – do something about it. But don't be drawn into an endless round of Fad diets. Quick weight loss will almost certainly lead to you being fatter when the weight goes back on. In fact, if you're a regular dieter, your size is often proportional to the number of Fad diets you've been on. This is because a lot of so-called Fad/Wonder Diets reduce muscle tissue instead of fat. And then, when you start eating normally, it is fat, not muscle, that goes back on. The only sure way to diet is to reduce your calorie intake. A high protein diet, plus exercise, will normally reduce weight steadily and keep it off, as long as you don't go back to stuffing your face. A final word of warning: avoid fancy diet preparations. The only thing that will wind up several pounds lighter is your wallet! (**SEE ALSO: YOU ARE WHAT YOU EAT, PEER PRESSURE, RIP-OFFS**)

DISCO: WHAT IS IT? *(Diss-Co: Wotizzit?):* Many years ago, before the invention of the record player, the local inhabitants of a village or town would gather after dark, and dance in a wild and frenzied manner, usually after they had consumed vast quantities of home-brewed Hamster Scrumpy. The music they danced to was Live, loud and incomprehensible, and played by local musicians, usually after *they* had consumed vast quantities of home-brewed Hamster Scrumpy. Occasionally a group of lads and their girls would turn up from a rival town, and the whole thing would turn into a punch-up. Hardly any of the organizers would notice that fighting had broken out, as the fighting and dancing looked very similar to the untrained eye. The whole ritual would end with the customary Last Dance, followed by the ritual Snogging, and then everyone would try to remember how to get home. This

Happening was called the Local Dance or the Local Hop (since the dancing consisted mostly of hopping about, due to the lack of space). This was, of course, in those far-off, unsophisticated times before Thomas Edison invented the phonograph. Now there was a brilliant man, even if he didn't know that the proper name for his invention was The Stereo Stacking System. So, how did this invention revolutionize the Local Hop? It didn't. The event has remained exactly the same, except that now the music was on disc. Hence the name – Disco. Oh, of course there have been tiny changes, mainly connected with local folklore and tradition more than anything else. For example, there is the fabled Handbag Dance. This is a totally feminist activity, involving a group of females dancing around their handbags. This dates back to the time when local hops were frequented by Cut-purses and Vagabonds, intent on stealing people's valuables. Nowadays the Cut-purse has been replaced by the Soccer Hooligan and the Lager Lout, neither of whom are interested in stealing people's money. They're far more concerned with thumping each other. (SEE ALSO: YOUR OWN DISCO, IMPRESSING YOUR DATE, BUNCH OF FIVES, ACID HOUSE PARTIES)

DOCTOR: JOB OPPORTUNITY (Doc-ter: Gob-opper Tune-Itty): Very similar to a Dentist, but the job takes in the whole body, not just the mouth. Ideal job for anyone who likes meeting people and telling them to take their clothes off. There's another bonus to this career: If you're a Doctor you can park more-or-less anywhere without getting clamped. On the negative side though, most of the people you meet do tend to have something wrong with them, and very often they want you to tell them what it is. This does mean that you need some skill. The basic requirements of the job are a reasonable working knowledge of the human body, and terrible hand-writing. However, if a patient comes to you with some complaint that you can't diagnose, the best thing to do is send them off with a very large bottle of pills. This will keep them amused for days, just trying to get the child-proof lid off. (**SEE ALSO: RECEPTIONIST, DENTIST, A VISIT TO THE DOCTOR'S**)

DRINK AND DRUGS *(Drinkndrugz):* The drink and drug problem is far more widespread than any of us realize. After all, everyone drinks. If you didn't you'd dehydrate. And many of the drinks we take contain drugs. Tea contains tannin, and coffee contains caffein. I try not to think about what tap water contains! Although caffeine and tannin are drugs, they are socially acceptable. After all, drug abuse is generally assoc-iated with *anti-social* behaviour, whereas no one ever started a riot after drinking tea, or gate-crashed a coffee morning. As far as we know, anyway! Alcohol is a different matter. It's readily available, and more socially acceptable than heroin, which is illegal. However, because the drinking of alcohol is socially acceptable, alcohol abuse is far more widespread than heroin abuse. The short answer to the problem is . . . er . . . if I knew that, it wouldn't be a problem, would it? (**SEE ALSO: ACID HOUSE PARTIES**)

E

EATING OUT *(EE-Ting Owt):* Eating out is a very good way of entertaining your date. Particularly if you have funny eating habits – that should keep them entertained for hours! Actually, when you consider that eating is something that we all do at least twice a day (in some cases much much more than twice!) (**SEE ALSO: FAT: AM I?, DIETING**), it is surprising just how fraught we can get in a restaurant. Of course, one of the reasons is the formality of the occasion. There are always far more knives and forks than you could possibly need, unless of course you were using them properly. Usually the only way you find out that you've used the wrong cutlery is when you get to the pudding, and you've only got a fish knife left. To make matters worse, waiters have a habit of hanging around and smiling at you. Just when you're trying to work out what all the different knives and things actually *do*. I can remember being in a restaurant once and spending hours trying to calculate how to make sure that I used each piece of cutlery at least once, only to discover that the table had accidentally been set for a party of twelve. Fortunately I was on my own at the time. This never happens at MacDonald's of course. There, they don't care which finger you stick in the sauce. But you can't go to MacDonald's for the rest of your life. Not if you're hoping to rise up the social ladder.

Eating Out is an essential part of many people's working life (not to mention love life!), and it could be of yours, so you'll need to get it right. So. The trick with the knives, forks, etc., is to start at the outside of the place setting, and work inwards. That way you can't go wrong, as long as the waiter has set it correctly. If you have anything left over at the end of the meal, you can always slip it into your pocket. If there are any strange implements that you cannot work out a use for, then the best thing to do is to hand them to the waiter, saying: "I ordered the Lobster, not the Lobotomy!" This will go down particularly well with waiters who speak no English. There are other simple ground rules. For instance: in a Chinese restaurant, don't try and eat the soup with chopsticks, unless you've got nothing to do for a few weeks.

The Menu: This is always a source of great panic, particularly when it's in a foreign language. This is made more complicated if you're in a French restaurant, and the menu is in Italian. Not that it will make any difference. The number of waiters who can understand the menu can be counted on one hand. Anyway, let's assume that you've coped with the menu and ordered your meal. Don't feel, just because the meal cost you all your Saturday job earnings from the last three years, that you have to eat everything. Leave something. Like the plate. Oh, and make sure that the waiter sees you leaving a tip, so that he/she can pick it up before one of the other diners does. Actually, don't feel obliged to leave a tip, especially if the service was bad. Most of the vegetables being served straight into your lap would constitute bad service. As would the waiter setting fire to your clothes instead of Flambé-ing your steak. One final word of warning: if you discover that you're a few pounds short for the bill, don't mention it until they've given you your coat back. **(SEE ALSO: IMPRESSING YOUR DATE, WAITERS, VESTS, SWEAT)**

ENDANGERED SPECIES *(End-ainjerd Speeseez):* For years conservationists have been appearing on TV, waving their arms about, and telling us to save a different species of animal. One week it's the whale, the next it's the elephant. I'm sick of it. I start saving whales, and just when I've got a decent collection, they tell me they want me to save something else. But if people didn't go around killing these animals, my garden shed wouldn't be packed with saved ones. So why do people kill them? One reason is sport. A sort of non-competitive sport, where the only loser is the animal, but he's not actually playing so he doesn't count. Then there's food, which doesn't really explain killing elephants or rhinos. (Mind you, how are we to know what's in those burgers? It's tough enough to be rhino!) At one time people used to kill stags. But I think this was only so that their heads could be mounted on walls, so that comedians could look at them and say, "Cor! He must have been travelling pretty fast!" Yes! That was a

joke! Now you know why Music Hall is as dead as a do-do! Perhaps in years to come, elephants will only exist in jokes. For example: how many Elephants does it take to change a light-bulb? Only one, but unless you ask him soon, I doubt he'll be available. (**SEE ALSO: BUILT-IN OBSOLESCENCE, BEAUTY WITHOUT CRUELTY, VEGGIES**)

EXERCISE *(X-er-size):* There's not a great deal to say about exercise except that, unless you are extremely fit, it's better not even to attempt it. The road to health is paved with dead joggers. (**SEE ALSO: SPORT, COMPETITION**)

F

FAME *(Phame):* Andy Warhol once said: "Everyone is famous for fifteen minutes." This could be true, who knows? If it is, you just have to hope that *your* fifteen minutes of fame don't happen during the night when you're fast asleep. Of course, fame can simply mean loss of privacy and having your dustbins searched by journalists from the Popular Dailies. The local cats are always going through my bins. But who knows, they could be very small *Sun* journalists in cat-skins. (**SEE ALSO: SUN, KEEPING PETS, POP FAME**)

FASHION: WHAT IS IT? *(Fascon: Wotizzit?):* If you live long enough, you'll see every type of outfit come back into fashion – even flares! This is not necessarily a good reason for hanging on to your old clothes, however. But what exactly *is* fashion? Who decides what's *in* and what's *out*? Well, it's possible, you think, that the people who buy clothes are the ones who set the trends. *Wrong!* It's the people who design and make the clothes who tell us what to wear – the big fashion houses, and the media. For example: the Media image-makers create an image for some pop band, and within minutes the High Street stores are selling look-a-like outfits. (**SEE ALSO: WANNA-BEES**) Occasionally the band flops, then so do the clothes, but usually it works very well. However, before you rush out and buy the outfit favoured by your Pop Idol, the thing to remember is this: that outfit was designed specifically for your Pop Idol, to make them look The Biz. It may not work quite so well on you! So don't be too surprised if, instead of looking like Bros, you end up looking like a bag of sprouts. Actually, that's a bad example. (**SEE ALSO: PEER PRESSURE**)

FASHION SLAVE *(Fash-Un Slaiv):* Someone who pursues

the latest fashion with the same tireless passion that Joan Collins pursues Youth (any youth, even one called Colin!). This passion can be fruitless (not to say costly), since many fashions don't really last long enough for you to get the clothes back from the shop. **(SEE ALSO: FASHION, RIP-OFFS)**

FAT: AM I? *(Phat: am-eye?):* Fatness, obesity – or to give it its correct medical name, *Corlookathestateovim* (male) or *Corlookathestateover* (female) – is relative. And by the same token, some relatives are fat. It can be dangerous to consider yourself fat, just because you are bigger than any of your friends. Maybe they are too thin. However, you should be able to tell by looking in the mirror whether you are fat or not. Use a full-length mirror. If you can see yourself from top to bottom

but not from side to side, chances are that you're fat. The best thing to do then is either to diet or to move further away from the mirror (you're bound to get all of your reflection in eventually!). But you must be honest with yourself. Ask yourself: Do chairs break when I sit on them? Can I get through doors? Does the school bus tip up when I board it? Here is a simple chart that you can use as a guideline:

Height	Ideal Weight (Female)	Ideal Weight (Male)
5'1"	44–49 kg	48–53 kg
5'2"	45–50 kg	49–56 kg
5'3"	47–51 kg	52–58 kg
5'4"	49–56 kg	54–60 kg
5'6"	53–59 kg	59–64 kg
5'8"	56–63 kg	62–69 kg

You've probably noticed a pattern emerging (paisley, I think it is). You can allow roughly 2 kg weight gain per inch of height gain. Which, in simple terms, means that if you are 102 kg (16 stone), you're not overweight so long as you are 7 feet 5 inches tall. (**SEE ALSO: DIETING, PEER PRESSURE**)

FISHING: HOBBY (*Fishin: Hobbie*): A jerk on one end of a line, waiting for a jerk on the other. (**SEE ALSO: HOBBIES, STAMP COLLECTING, COIN COLLECTING**)

FOLK MUSIC (*Foke-mewzik*): Of all forms of music, Folk Music is perhaps the oldest. It is certainly the one that gets the micky taken out of it the most. But what is it? Well, basically, it was the earliest form of newspaper. Before

the printing press was invented, before TV came on the scene, the only way people could find out the news was by word of mouth. Someone, probably a medieval Stock Aitken and Waterman, turned newsworthy events into songs. For example, take the exploits of the famous highwayman, Dick Turpin: The number of folk songs written about his adventures must run into, ooh, several. A typical stanza might go:

(1) Oh, bold Dick Turpin he was a lad,
(2) With a Hi, and a Ho, and Riddle-me-dee,
(3) The things he did were terrible bad,
(4) With a Hi-Fi, Scooby-Doo,
(5) And bonny sweet Beryl is all my joy.

Lines 2, 4 and 5 would be repeated every verse, so you can see that the narrative would develop very, very slowly. This obviously made the songs very long indeed. And, since people in those days rarely lived past 40, they hardly ever got to hear the end of the song. Thus legends were born, as people speculated on the outcome of the song. History doesn't relate who *Beryl* was, but it was probably the songwriter's sweetheart, landlady or agent. This type of music is favoured by Anoraxia sufferers, Train Spotters and Real Ale drinkers. (**SEE ALSO: ANORAXIA**)

FOOTBALL: SPORT *(Futborl: Spawt):* Traditionally Football was a village game, with very few rules, played by as many people as cared to join in. A dangerous "sport", it was basically a free-for-all and a great chance to settle old scores and let off steam. In fact, it was banned in Cromwellian times for being ungodly. It's surprising how little it's changed, really! (**SEE ALSO: SPORT, COMPETITION, CRICKET, SNOOKER, WIMBLEDON**)

FOREIGN LANGUAGES *(For-in Langwidges):* It is when you're in a fancy restaurant, with the person of your dreams, staring at the menu, or on a day trip to Bologne (*not* pronounced Bol-Ogny, by the way), trying to impress your date, that you wish you'd paid more attention in French lessons. I didn't do French at school. I did German. I suppose that was just in case they declared war on us again. But the German language has been of no use to me, except for hanging on to my deckchair on holiday. (The way to do this, incidentally, is to say: "Das ist meine Bleischtift!" Actually I think that probably means Fountain Pen or Gall Bladder, but they'll get the idea if you look mean enough.) My daughter is learning Spanish. Again, not a lot of use at the moment, but I think it'll come in handy for all those 18 to 30 holidays on the Costa Packet. Already she is concentrating all her energies into phrases like "Leave that bull alone", "Do you sell low-alcohol Harvey Wallbangers?", and "If you pinch my bum again, Pedro, I'll deck you!" (SEE ALSO: AUSTRALIAN, BUNCH OF FIVES) I think that'll probably cover just about anything that's likely to happen to her out there! Of course, there's always been a very British assumption that everyone else speaks English. In fact, in many countries they do, extremely well. But that usually only serves to remind you how little effort you made to learn their language. And, with 1992, the united Europe and single market only two years away, those of us who are monolingual are going to get caught with our trousers down, and we won't even be able to say it in French!

FORMING A BAND *(4 minga band):* The very first thing you must do when forming a band is to find some other members. You can't form a band on your own. Obviously it's handy if you've got a few pals who fancy being in a band, but it is still possible to get a band together if you haven't got a friend in the world. (SEE: BODY ODOUR) Selecting the people for your band can be very important. It's a question of image. For instance, try and get them all with the right-length hair (this way you won't have to waste your limited funds on hair-styling). Similarly, try to get people with the right clothes, etc. A tip here: you would be very unwise to have anyone in your band who is better looking than you. If you are no oil painting (ie: very ugly), it might be an idea to consider putting together a Heavy Metal band. That way it won't matter if the collective beauty of the band is enough to curdle milk.

You'll notice that, so far, I have made no mention of musical instruments. This is because I don't want you to get the idea that they are in any way a priority. Get your line-up right first. You'll have plenty of time to worry about which of you is going to hold which instrument on *Top of the Pops* later. Another tip: make sure that at least one member of the band has very wealthy parents. If possible, wealthy and generous, although these qualities don't often go together. It will help you in the long run if this particular band member is the least musically

G

GAME SHOWS *(Gaim-Shoze):* Every other programme on TV is a Game Show. Many of these originate in America, where the prizes are worth winning! Not so in this country. In the UK there are very strict controls over how much you can win. Whereas in America you can win a house, a million dollars, or even a new (or secondhand) wife/husband, here the most you can get is £4,000 or a Skoda. Actually, one of the most popular prizes in English TV is a piece of reproduction Regency furniture. Who wants to win that? Unless your

house is stuffed with reproduction Regency furniture, it's going to look really out of place, isn't it? Also, I can't personally imagine anyone who has a passion for reproduction Regency furniture allowing themselves to be seen *dead* on a Game Show, can you? (Oh! That's just given me a great idea for a Game Show! It's called *Name That Stiff*, and it involves people being seen dead on TV. I'll have to flesh it out a bit, but I'm sure it'll catch on. Yes, of course it's tasteless, but I doubt that anyone will notice!) Mind you, the prizes are no worse than the games themselves. What do we have on offer?

Bob's Full House, in which people compete to try and get the audience to shout out "Droopy Drawers", in order to win a matching set of reproduction Regency Bath-Towels.

That's My Dog, in which dog-owners compete to prevent their mutt from watering the set, in order to win reproduction Regency Dog Biscuits.

Family Fortunes, in which two families, often only related by marriage and clearly hating each other, compete to see which bunch can look the biggest Plonkers in the space of thirty minutes, and predict what the hundred people surveyed said they were most likely to call out if they heard their next-door neighbour redecorating his back bedroom at four in the morning. All this for the (dubious) pleasure of being cuddled by Les Dennis! (I know he isn't exactly reproduction Regency, but I'm sure he's got Queen Anne's legs.)

Frankly, I'm surprised that no one has hit on the idea of Religious Game Shows. After all, we live in an age when nothing is sacred. (SEE ALSO: ACTS OF GOD, GODS, TV PRESENTER (CHILDREN'S))

GET STUCK IN!: EXPRESSION *(Getz-tuckin: X-preshon):* Find yourself in the unfortunate position of being unable either to remove something from your person, or to remove your person from something. Can refer to sticky substances, such as quicksand, eight-foot bowls of school custard, etc.

GETTING A JOB *(Jet in a gob):* There's a great deal of hysterical talk these days about the lack of available work, three million unemployed, etc., etc. But applying for a job could not be easier. All you need to do is go into your nearest Job Centre and say: "I'd like a Job, please", and they'll tell you exactly where to go. (**SEE ALSO: ACCOUNTANT, DOCTOR, HIGH COURT JUDGE, ETC**)

GETTING OUT OF GAMES *(ge-ting O-toff Gaimz):* The traditional method, and the one recognized by most of the Teaching Unions, is to bring a Note. Although the Note is traditionally forged, you can bring one from your parents, but this is usually considered rather *wimpish*. The best Note is the (forged) one with only the vaguest attempts at joined-up writing. Remember, if you make it look too well written, no teacher will ever believe that your parents wrote it. Particularly if your parents were pupils at the same school. The odd spelling mistake usually helps, but again don't try and be too clever. Avoid literary puns, quotations from Shakespeare, or jokes that rely on a knowledge of syntax, as the teacher will almost certainly not understand them. After all, this is the Games Teacher we're dealing with, and Games Teachers are not noted for their command of the English language (or indeed their command of the rules of any known sport). One final word of warning: when signing the note, don't use your own name. Oh, and *never, never* sign the note: "Yours sincerely, My Mum". Even a Games Teacher would spot that as a sign of a forgery. (**SEE ALSO: AVOIDING SHOWERS**)

GODS *(Godz):* The world is made up of many nationalities, colours and creeds. Consequently there are various different gods. This is nothing new. In the ancient world there were many gods, some of whom had days named after them. For example, Thursday is named after Thor, the Norse God of Thunder, Wednesday is named after Woden, the Norse God of Window Dressers, and Friday is named after Fryin, the Norse God of Fish. This explains why we eat fish on Fridays, and monks are called *Friars*, even if they're not Norwegian. But there are more religions than gods. This is because many religions worship the same god. In fact, most religious wars down the centuries have been between different factions of the same religion. Which is odd, really, because they're on the same side – aren't they? Clearly it's not only gods that move in mysterious ways! (**SEE ALSO: ACTS OF GOD, JEHOVAH'S WITNESSES**)

GO FOR IT!: EXPRESSION *(Go-4-itt: X-preshon):* Fetch it! Quite a handy command when exercising the dog with a stick. That is to say, not hitting the dog with a stick, but throwing the stick and commanding the dog to fetch it. Although, of course, dogs are not noted for their extreme intelligence, so it might be quicker to threaten to hit the dog with the stick, unless he fetches it. Or to tell the dog to fetch the stick, so that you can hit him with it, or . . . I think it might be quicker to get a cat! (**SEE ALSO: KEEPING PETS, ROTTWEILERS**)

GOING GREEN *(Gow-ing Green):* Becoming Environmentally Friendly. Refusing to do anything that might damage the Ozone Layer, even if you don't know what the Ozone Layer is. This usually involves checking cans of hairspray for the little Ozone Friendly sticker, while still eating Burgers that cost half a Tropical Rainforest to produce. Unfortunately, the process of persuading people to Go Green is slowed down quite considerably by the image that the term Green has. For generations, Green has been associated with cabbage, cooked to loving death by armies of Dinner Ladies the world over. (**SEE ALSO: OZONE LAYER, GREENHOUSE EFFECT, SCHOOL DINNERS**)

GREAT SCRABBLE CONSPIRACY: THE *(Grate Scrabbul-Con-spearer-see: thee):* Elsewhere in this book I have pointed out that there are various new words in common usage these days which do not, on the face of it, have any real meaning. But they all have one thing in common. They all provide a really good score in Scrabble. This suggests to me a Great Conspiracy, by the inventors of these words (Mediafolk, without a doubt) to improve their Scrabble chances. Anyone who has ever played Scrabble will know how difficult it is to get rid of a high-scoring letter, such as a Z. At least, it *was*, until Zany and Zappy came on the scene. Not to mention Wacky. What amazes me is that no one has so far come up with a trendy, meaningless word that uses a *Q* without the obligatory *U*. But they're probably working on it. What's more, the people who decide what goes into dictionaries are obviously in on the Scam, because these words are appearing in dictionaries the length and breadth of the UK. Where will it stop? I imagine it will continue until it is impossible to have a rational conversation with anyone other than a Scrabble player. That's going to count me out for a start!

GREENHOUSE EFFECT: WHAT IS IT? *(Grean-hows-F-ekt: Wotizzit?):* There is increasing concern about the state of our planet. One of the things that people are getting more and more concerned about is Global Warming, or The Greenhouse Effect. The Greenhouse Effect was first noticed by scientists as far back as the 1860s. Margaret Thatcher had just been born, and Cliff Richard was in the hit parade. As always, no one believed the scientists any more than they believed them when the scientists said that the earth was round, or that blood was pumped around the body by the heart, and didn't just sit in your legs, waiting to fall out if you cut your foot. Now, of course, people are realizing that the scientists are right, which means that the situation is obviously a lot worse than we can imagine. So, what is it all about? The earth is surrounded by an Ozone Layer. Ozone is pure oxygen, and the Ozone Layer filters out harmful ultra-violet rays from the sun. But, because of Chlorofluorocarbons (CFCs) in aerosol sprays, foam packaging and refrigerator coolant, holes are appearing in the Ozone Layer and letting through the ultra-violet rays, which, in turn, are heating up the atmosphere, rather like being in a greenhouse.

So, why are people so reluctant to act? Well, if I tell you that the Greenhouse Effect means that the oceans are getting warmer and the climate generally is getting hotter, then you can see why people, in this country at least, would be very reluctant to do anything. After all, we don't get any decent weather as a rule, and the seas around England are enough to freeze a jolly good fellow. So it would be hard to persuade your average Brit that the long hot summer of 1989 was in fact a bad sign, particularly if he or she is still nursing a great

tan. Not to mention the effects on the crops. The farmers must be over the moon. Try telling them that the hot weather is bad for us. So, the bad news is that we're all going to fry, but the good news is that the tomatoes have never been bigger! **(SEE ALSO: OZONE LAYER)**

H

HAIRDRESSER: HOW TO BECOME ONE *(Hare-Dressa: How-2B-Cum-1):* It isn't difficult. I mean, anyone who can operate a pair of scissors without actually cutting their own arm off should be able to cut hair. Cutting it properly is a different matter. But someone once said: "Where there's a will, there's a way", although they never actually explained what it meant. But the trick is not to let the client (the person getting their hair cut) see the results of your handiwork. So, no mirrors. Anywhere. Not even in the loos. Then, if they come back to complain, you can always say that the wind must have blown it out of shape. Of course, washing hair will always cover up the badly cut bits. This may explain why hairdressers wash hair before they cut it – they already know from experience which bits they are going to cut badly!

HERBALISM: WHAT IS IT? *(Herbble-Ism: Wotizzit?):* There has been a lot of talk recently about herbalism and alternative medicine. Even Prince Charles, the future King of England, has become interested in it. So, what is herbalism? Well, since it is obviously going to replace conventional medicine once Charles comes to the throne, it would be as well to know something about it. Actually this could explain why many people have started questioning whether we really need a constitutional monarch. They obviously realize that the minute Charles takes over, the health service will switch to alternative medicine. Maybe they are afraid that their doctor will make them go around with a bit of seaweed strapped to their kneecap, instead of just taking a couple of paracetamol. But what are these herbs, and what do they do? Well, obviously the different types are as many and varied as drugs down a disco toilet during a police raid. And, in common with the current drugs, many of these herbs are virtually impossible to obtain and will do you no good if you do get hold of them. But here is a quick guide to the ones in more common usage:

Name: Wirtbane

Appearance: Small, purple-and-white-striped flower. Invisible leaves.

Where found: On the hard shoulders of partly-built motorways.

Application: Should be crushed and lightly simmered over a beechwood fire for three weeks, then added to boiling water and inhaled through the nozzle of a Dr Cobblers' Aromatic

Inhaler (no longer made, but can still be found in some antique shops and on un-redeveloped World War Two bomb sites). Inhalation should be performed under a muslin or fine Indian silk headscarf for thirty minutes in a darkened room.

Usage: A thirty-minute inhalation of the steam from crushed Wirtbane will induce in the patient a feeling of complete pointlessness. Particularly good for people who are bored and can't think of anything better to do.

Name: Devil's Nostril

Not, obviously, its real name. It is common practice amongst herbalists to give plants "nicknames" suggested by their appearance. The plant's real name is Gypsy's Buttock.

Appearance: Devil's Nostril takes its name from the fact that it looks exactly like the left windscreen wiper of a Ford Cortina. Only different.

Where found: On the beds of rivers, especially very deep ones. Some scuba-diving experience is useful when looking for this particular plant.

Application: Crushing the stem between the thumb and index finger of either hand will cause a magenta-coloured sap to be released. It will also cause a very nasty skin rash that is virtually impossible to get rid of, except by asking a conventional doctor for a very long, strong course of antibiotics. The sap should be applied to the lobes of each ear, and the widow's peak, if you have one. If you haven't got a widow's peak, then a divorcee's peak, a jilted sweetheart's peak, or even a stood-up girlfriend's peak might do just as well. A fit of pique wouldn't be any use at all.

Usage: This particular herb is extremely good for loneliness, due to its extremely vile smell. One application should ensure that you will be lonely for as long as it lasts (which is usually the rest of your life).

Naturally I cannot list all the hundreds of available herbs and plants, as space is very limited here. For further information you could get a copy of *Old Crumbly's Book of Herbal Cures*. It has been out of print for about 300 years, but I would imagine that most health-food shops will have plenty of copies in stock. However, if you feel that you don't want to try to buy the book, just in case you can't get it and feel that the sense of disappointment might be too great, here are a few "Off The Shelf" remedies that you might like to try:

Puckle seeds: Very good for removing unsightly navel hair.
Ferret thistle: Cures athlete's foot.
Dock root: Cures vomiting, but it's very hard to keep down.

Bog myrtle: Very good for diarrhoea, if you like having diarrhoea, that is. (**SEE ALSO: DOCTOR, A VISIT TO THE DOCTOR**)

HIGH COURT JUDGE: JOB OPPORTUNITY *(Hi-caught judge: Gob-Opper Tune-Itty):* A men-only job, I'm afraid, but a great one for anyone who likes dressing up in wigs and frocks. (**SEE ALSO: BARRISTER**) Very similar to the job of Pantomime Dame, although a judge is not often required to dance, sing or do comedy cookery scenes. Mind you, many High Court Judges will confirm that these are useful additional skills, especially for the longer trials. And this is one of the drawbacks of the job. Many trials go on for months. So long, in fact, that very often the judge has forgotten what the prisoner was originally charged with. For this reason judges often decide in advance what verdict they are going to give, and even what sentence, and then fall asleep for the duration of the trial. This can of course backfire if you're not careful. There was once a case of a judge who decided beforehand to sentence the criminal to deportation to Australia. At the

A high court judge

end of the trial he passed sentence, only to discover that, during the course of the trial, deportation had been abolished. Having passed sentence he was unable to change it, so he saved face by commuting the sentence to a fortnight's holiday on the Great Barrier Reef. The only major requirement for this job is that you need to be very very old indeed. It is not therefore the sort of job you can jump straight into on leaving school. However, you could fill in the time by doing Further Education. Unfortunately this will give you the positive disadvantage of being over-qualified. (**SEE ALSO: SPEAKER – HOUSE OF COMMONS, GETTING A JOB, RECEPTIONIST**)

HIRE PURCHASE: *(High-er-per-chus):* On the face of it, Hire Purchase should basically mean that you hire something, and at the end of the hire period, you discover that you have bought (or purchased) it. Yes. That's more-or-less right, in theory. In reality, the situation is not that simple. For *Hire*, read *Higher*. That is to say that the goods you are interested in buying will cost you more. You will pay a *higher* price for them. Now let's look at the word *Purchase*. Yes, it does mean *Buy*. But it also has another, more sinister meaning. *Purchase* also means: "a firm grip on something". And that's exactly what happens. As soon as you sign a Hire Purchase agreement, the Credit Company who have offered you the agreement have a firm (and binding) hold on you until you finish paying. It's very complicated. It's all to do with a thing called APR, which I think probably stands for : "All Prices Raised" but I might be wrong. All I know is that Hire Purchase means that you'll pay for it, and they won't let you off until you've coughed up. Still, it might be better than not owning the thing at all! Purchase is a word that has passed out of common usage, probably because it gives a really pathetic score in Scrabble.

HOBBIES: WHAT ARE THEY? *(Hob-eez: Wot-R-thay?):* Well, of course, a Hobby can be almost anything that you do in your spare time. However, this doesn't include sitting around, bored out of your brain, wondering what to do *with* your spare time. It could include Stamp Collecting, Beer Mat Collecting (unless this involves sniffing the Beer Mats, which would take the pastime out of the realms of "Hobby", and into that of "Drink Problem"), Tea-Bag Card Collecting, in fact collecting almost anything. Almost. But not quite. For instance, Collecting Dust could not really be considered a hobby, unless you're a chair. Although I suppose it does depend on how you do it. Of course, nowadays the manufacturers have very kindly made things much easier for collectors. They have invented a product called the Collectable. (**SEE ALSO: COLLECTABLES**) Keeping a pet could be considered a hobby. Consistently forgetting to clean it out couldn't. (**SEE ALSO: KEEPING PETS**) Many sports are considered hobbies – rather sadistic forms of hobby, but hobbies nonetheless. (**SEE ALSO: SPORT**)

HOSPITAL FOOD – WHAT IS IT? *(Hors-Pittal Fude: Wotizzit?):* Difficult to tell. Certainly looking at it gives no obvious clues. I have to confess that I have never personally sampled it. Mainly because I have never stayed in hospital long enough to qualify for a meal (three days is the longest I've ever been hospitalized). But I know a man who has. In fact I know many people who have had relatives in hospital. And almost all of them, when they phoned up to see how their particular kin was doing, were told: "They passed away peacefully – just after lunch." Just after lunch! There's got to be a connection! Sounds very ominous to me. I think if I ever did stay in hospital for any length of time, and they came round with the lunch menu, I would insist that they also showed me the list of that morning's operations. Then, if there had been any organ removals (particularly livers or kidneys), I would insist that they served me a plain green salad (with no avocado). I have heard, although it may not be true, that some hospitals are so short-staffed that some junior surgeons also work in the kitchens.

66

I wonder how many fatalities hospital catering staff have to have to their credit, before they get promoted to doing school dinners? I do happen to know that, in the old days, nurses used to practise giving injections by sticking needles into oranges. Whether these oranges were then sold to an unsuspecting public I really

don't know. But that could explain why parents are always saying that oranges are good for you: not only do they contain lots of vitamin C, but they also give you instant immunity to 57 different varieties of rare tropical disease. So, although an apple a day keeps the doctor away, an orange a day keeps Ugandan Belly, Trench Foot, Murphy's Blight, Thatcher's Mouth, and all manner of dreaded lurgies at bay. Who knows, it may even give you the ability to write a best-selling novel.

(SEE: JEFFREY ARCHER, SCHOOL DINNERS)

I

IDOLS *(Idlz):* These are people, figures, pop stars, footballers, and anyone else who is looked up to by the likes of you and me. They are called Idols because of the one thing they all have in common – they don't do much work! (**SEE ALSO: FAME**)

IMPRESSING YOUR DATE *(Im-pressing yor dait):* Lesson one in impressing your date is to get off on the right foot. This is particularly important if you're going dancing (although some dances demand that you get off on the left foot). It's even more important if you're going marching, although this doesn't make for a particularly exciting evening out, unless you're both really into that sort of thing. Begin as you mean to go on, and the best way to begin a successful evening out is to turn up. That always goes down well. Unless, of course, they're going out with you because they didn't have the heart to say *no*, in which case you will impress them much more if you *don't* turn up. How you find out before the date is another matter . . . (**SEE ALSO: DATES**) Having turned up, you will score even more points if you have made an effort with your appearance. For example:

Boys: Your date will really be impressed if you have put on a clean shirt. Had a shower. Dried yourself. Dried the shirt. Ironed the shirt. Taken the shirt off and treated the burns to your chest and back. Replaced the shirt again. Left the house in plenty of time to catch the bus. Returned home again to put on your trousers, jacket, socks, shoes, etc. A small gift wouldn't go amiss. It's old-fashioned, I know, but not soppy. Sweets are a good choice, and chocolates rather than gob-stoppers. Particularly if she hasn't got her own teeth. (**SEE ALSO: DENTIST**)

Girls: Dress up, but don't overdo it, or you might embarrass your date. After all, the smartest thing he has in the clothes line might be his school uniform. The same applies to perfume. A little drop goes a long way. Remember that some perfumes are very provocative, which is another word for expensive. Avoid perfumes with names like Burning Passion, Unbridled Lust, or All-in Wrestling on the Back Row of the Pictures, unless that's the sort of date you're looking for.

This is probably as good a point as any to point out that many lads seem to think that unless they jump on you you'll think they're boring. You, on the other hand, may well be looking forward to watching a film you've wanted to see for weeks, having a good chat about it, then rounding off the evening with a burger, a coffee, and a walk to the bus station. Unfortunately there are chaps who believe that it's no use trying to have a conversation with a girl, because girls' ears don't work properly until they've been nibbled a bit. One way of putting a stop to this is to put a few drops of nailbite on each ear lobe. That should do the trick! Of course, if you think you might need something stronger, then make yourself some earrings out of cotton wool balls. Then, if the Nibbler is getting out of hand, excuse yourself, pop into the Ladies, and dip your earrings in Ether. That'll have him comatose in no time. An added bonus of this is that he'll probably dream that he's having a brilliant time! So, having selected your outfit, the low-cut black number or the full suit of armour and cotton wool ball earrings, you're ready to impress your date.

Both: Of course, neither sex should ever let on that they've made a great effort, particularly if their date can't stand them!

Conversation: This can so easily flag, particularly if you *do* discover that you can't stand the sight of each other. However, assuming that you are still talking, a well-chosen remark (or even compliment) will definitely score you points. But be careful. Suit the remark to the moment and venue. For example:

At The Cinema:

Don't say: "Are you still there?"

Do say: "Are you enjoying the film?" However, if they say "Yes", *don't* say: "Oh. It must be someone else snoring, then!"

At a Football Match:

Don't say: "Hold this bog roll while I smack this bloke in the gob!" (very unladylike!), or "Shout at the ref for me, will you? Your mouth's bigger than mine!" (very ungentlemanly!)

A nice thing for you to say, if you're a guy is: "You look great!" If she says: "Thanks", don't add: "Yeah, even better than Maradonna!"

At The Disco:

Say anything as long as it's loud.

In a Restaurant:

This is probably the most romantic place you can go with someone on a date. Consequently it lends itself to the well-chosen romantic remark. But don't blow it. Don't say: "I'd better not have the peas, they'll make me fart." If you're a chap, look deeply into your partner's eyes, and mutter something along the lines of: "You look so beautiful with the candle-light dancing in your hair – it almost seems a pity to call the fire brigade." (**SEE ALSO: EATING OUT, WAITERS, SWEAT, VESTS, MAKING YOUR OWN CLOTHES, FASHION SLAVE, FASHION**)

INSULTS: DEALING WITH (in-salts: D-lingwith): In an argument, nothing squashes an opponent more quickly than a well-thought out, well-turned phrase. The kind of biting wit that Oscar Wilde would have gone to gaol for, or Shakespeare would have given his right arm for (or at least his non-writing arm), or Esau would have swapped for a mess of pottage, whatever that is! That caustic quip that makes even the sharpest raconteur jump to his or her feet in spontaneous appreciation. The sort of stuff that makes Ruth Laurence* look like RodneyTrotter. So, what are they, these rapier-like jibes that can ensure complete victory in any argument? Well, I'm known for being pretty handy when it comes to withering verbals, and I'll happily share my secrets with you. Feel free to use these sharp and snappy replies at any time, and watch the opposition literally crumble before your eyes. My most successful lines are: "And you are!", "Shut your mouth!" and "You what?" I can also let you have the name of a very good

71

doctor, who can treat injuries received during arguments without leaving too much of a scar.

(*Ruth Laurence: That super-bright child who went to university at 12, and passed her doctorate at 15. I'd like to meet her, so I could ask her: "Why?") (**SEE ALSO: BUNCH OF FIVES**).

J

JASON DONOVAN: CONDITION *(Jayce-un Don-oven: Con-Dishun):* The condition of being in a state of continual amazement. One minute you're a Soap Star, then you're a Pop Star, then you're a Sex Symbol, then nobody knows who the hell you are. But the great thing about sufferers is that they manage to smile blandly throughout, giving them the appearance of knowing something that no one else does. This is, however, not the case. There is nothing they know that isn't already known by everyone else, even the humblest Cheesy-Bob (that's common usage for Woodlouse). **(SEE ALSO: KYLIE MINOGUE'S HAIRDRESSER, AUSTRALIAN)**

JAZZ: WHAT IS IT? *(Jaz: Wotizziyt?):* Free-form music, often played in jazz clubs. Because it is so free-form, it tends to go on and on, because no one really knows how to finish. What usually happens is that the drummer, realizing that it'll take him an hour to pack up his kit, and he's about to miss his last bus, suddenly hits everything in sight – drums, cymbals, customers, fellow musicians, etc. This is a fairly unsubtle way of telling the rest of the Musos to shut up. It doesn't always work, and it isn't unknown for fights to break out. The most famous British Jazz Club is called Ronnie Scott's, named after the first explorer ever to take a jazz band to the South Pole. **(SEE ALSO: FORMING A BAND, TOURING WITH YOUR BAND/ GROUP, NAMING YOUR BAND, BUNCH OF FIVES, HOSPITAL FOOD)**

JEFFREY ARCHER: WHAT IS HE? *(JEFF-re-ah Cher: Wotizzee?):* Extensive research reveals that he is in fact an author. I suspected something of the sort when I heard him say, on a TV chat show, that – and I quote – "Anyone can write a best-selling novel." This is something that you will probably find reassuring, particularly if you have just left school, have very few qualifications, and are wondering just what the heck you are going to do for a living. It must be even more reassuring to note that he didn't say anything about the best-selling novel being any good. (**SEE ALSO: GETTING A JOB; READ FOR RESEARCH ONLY:** FIRST AMONG EQUALS, CANE AND ABEL)

JEHOVAH'S WITNESSES *(Je-hoverz Wit-nis-iz):* Not everyone who knocks on your door is a Double Glazing Salesman. Occasionally it might be a friend paying you a visit, or the School Truant Officer trying to find out where you've been for the last five years. Or your visitor might be a Jehovah's Witness. It's hard to tell. I mean, they look and act perfectly normally. Very like Double Glazing Salesmen, in fact. But Jehovah's Witnesses are not trying to sell windows. In fact, they're not *selling* anything. They are offering you something, or at least they firmly believe they are. And yet they are the butt of more jokes than probably any other religious denomination, apart from Double Glazing Salesmen. Why? They don't try and rip you off, or go on the TV and tell

PLEASE COME OUT KEVIN... I'M NOT A JEHOVAH'S WITNESS, I'M YOUR MUM

you that you'll be damned for ever unless you send them all your money, like some American TV Evangelists. And yet they cause more people to put their necks out hiding under the stairs when the doorbell goes than even the bloke selling brushes. They've obviously got something. I wish I knew what it was. I do know that they're psychic, because they always know when you're in the bath. That's when they call round. Incidentally, the name Jehovah's Witness suggests that they have witnessed the Lord. Have actually seen, or even met, Him. If this is the case then I'm going to ask them what He thinks of the Channel Tunnel. (SEE ALSO: GODS, ACTS OF GOD, BUNCH OF FIVES, SELF DEFENCE, GAME SHOWS)

JOAN COLLINS: CONDITION *(Jone-Colin-z: Con-Dishun):* The unfortunate state of not being able to go anywhere or do anything without it getting into the papers. This condition is made all the worse by being self-inflicted. It also causes the sufferer to be told continually: "You look very very good for a fifty-year old." A fifty-year-old *what*, though? (SEE ALSO: TV PRESENTER (CHILDREN'S), FAME)

JOINED-UP WRITING *(Joyn-Dup Rye-Ting):* A sure-fire way of assessing someone's educational ability is their handwriting. Of course, doctors are the exception to the Golden Rule. Doctors have cultivated a way of writing that is indecipherable. This is so you cannot read what they've prescribed for you. The problem is that neither can the man in the chemist, which is why you never get any better. But Joined-Up Writing is a real gift; it will stand you in good stead for the rest of your life. For instance, if you can do JUW, as they say in educational circles, you'll be able to write autographs when you're a famous Rock Star, Footballer or Mass Murderer. Perhaps these are bad examples. I know! Master the art of JUW, and you'll be able to get a job as a secretary, and type everything! (SEE ALSO: SCHOOL: POINT OF, SCHOOL: AVOIDING, GETTING OUT OF GAMES)

K

KEEPING PETS *(Key-Ping Petz):* Everyone has a pet at some time in their life – dog, cat, goldfish, gerbil, hamster, armadillo, etc. But pet ownership is not something to be entered into lightly. Just before Christmas every year the campaign starts on TV, in magazines and on the radio. You'll have heard the slogan: "A Pet Is For Life, Not Just For Lunch." Well. Yes. It can be for life, I suppose. It depends whether you feed it or not. But the biggest problem with all pets is the fact that they are *animals*. And the big problem with animals is that they have little or no understanding of basic toilet-training. When God Made the Beasts of the Field, etc, it was probably the one thing he overlooked. But what do you expect in six days? Miracles? Of course, some effort has been made to redress the problem. Poop-Bins have been introduced for dogs, but they've all been erected far too high to be of any use to any dog smaller than a Rottweiler. This might explain the popularity of Rottweilers, although I doubt it somehow! **(SEE ALSO: ROTTWEILERS)**

The most embarrassing thing about owning a dog is when you are walking it through a park, and it suddenly decides that it's time to *go*. It's usually when you're standing within a couple of feet of an 84-piece Salvation Army band that plays so well that it has drawn a sizeable crowd.

And it doesn't stop at dogs. Rabbits, hamsters, mice, gerbils and budgies all have the same casual attitude towards Big Jobs. They've probably never even *heard* of an Avocado Bathroom Suite. **(SEE ALSO: AVOCADO)** Consequently they have to be cleaned out, regularly. This is one of the few things that Pet Shops never mention when they are twisting your arm to give a moth-eaten little gerbil a good home. But your parents never stop mentioning it. So you succumb to the nagging, and clean out the pet. Getting the pet to stand at one end of its cage while you shovel the "stuff" up is the first problem. Stopping it from standing in the "stuff" every time you stop shovelling to adjust the peg on your nose is the second problem. Finding cleverer and cleverer ways of avoiding doing the job at all is the third, fourth, fifth through to five hundred and eleventh problem.

Fish are just as bad. Mind you, who'd be a fish? Spending your whole life swimming around in your own toilet, with your mouth hanging open. "Have you cleaned your fish?" my mother always used to say to me. What did she mean? How do you clean a fish? With soap? A scrubbing brush? I tried a brillo pad once, but all I ended up with was a handful of scales and a very clean fish who spent the rest of his days floating around on the surface of his bowl. He went right off his food. Mind you, that made him very cheap to keep. Now that I'm famous, of course, I don't do any cleaning, not even of pets. I have a cleaner and the goldfish have a scuba diver who drops in twice a week. (**SEE ALSO: HOBBIES**)

KISSING: HOW? *(Kiss-in Howe?):* There is no one particular technique. But the biggest problem with kissing, certainly kissing someone for the first time, is where will everything go? By that I refer to arms, legs, Walkmans, or even cardboard pelican beaks if you're in fancy dress, etc. These sort of things are very unpredictable. I mean, you can't really say: "I'm going to kiss you now. OK? So would you like to tell me if you intend to make any sudden movements?" No, you can't really say that. It might be as well, though, to check if your date is given to involuntary spasms of any sort, or if they are particularly ticklish. But be subtle when finding out! Don't for instance, ask them for a list of their childhood diseases, or ask to see their medical card. Once you've ascertained that your intended victim has no nasty twitches or incurable diseases, the next thing to check is that they haven't got anything in their hands, such as ice cream, chocolates, knitting, a thirty-pound sledge-hammer or one end of a grand piano. Actually, a really bad time to start trying to kiss someone is when they are engaged in rearranging furniture, especially if you are at the other end of the very long sofa that they are currently lifting. Assuming that they have empty hands, and are in a kissable situation (sitting down next to you is good), then you are ready to proceed. Try to predict what will happen to their arms, hands etc. Obviously if they have some idea that they are about to be kissed, it helps. So get their attention. Look into their eyes. Not too long, otherwise they'll wonder what they've got hanging out of their nose. Move slowly forward.

Now is a good time for the chap to say something. Or the girl if she feels like it. But avoid speaking together. This only happens on TV, never in real life. Work out what you're going to say beforehand, otherwise you'll probably come out with something unromantic, like: "You haven't eaten garlic recently, have you?" What you say doesn't need to be fancy.

Avoid Shakespearian sonnets, for instance. Particularly if you want to kiss that same night. You should also avoid anything that sounds like a promise, especially if your date is the sort of person who might hold you to it, once you've chucked them. Chaps: Don't say "Has anyone ever told you that you're beautiful?" if she is. Because she'll reply, "Yes, loads of times", and that will kill the moment. Actually, don't say it if she's ugly either, because that could kill the whole evening. Say "I think you're beautiful", if you like, but just be careful which word you put the stress on! Then Go For It!

I think it's probably fair to assume that you and your date will both realize that we kiss on the lips in this country, otherwise there might be a terrible collision, as one of you goes for the hand and the other starts rubbing noses Eskimo-style. There is no set way to kiss. I imagine that, once your lips meet, the rest will take care of itself, but if you're unsure you can always have a St. John's Ambulance person standing by! One final word of warning: should you decide to kiss with your mouth open, do make sure that your date isn't eating at the time. Nothing takes the edge off a romantic moment more quickly than your date saying as you lean back feeling pleased with your kissing efforts, "Here! You've pinched my dill pickle!" Happy kissing! (**SEE ALSO: SPORT, DISCOS, BUNCH OF FIVES**)

KISSING: WHEN? *(Kiss-in: Wen?):* This is the big one. And, frankly, it's one that nobody really knows the answer to. It's that first kiss that is the most difficult to judge. But there are a few ground rules to be observed. For instance: before you plant that smacker that is going to make his or her toes curl up, make sure that you've been introduced. Nothing alarms a person more than suddenly being kissed by a total stranger. They may not find it altogether unpleasant, just unexpected.

But let's assume that you know the other person, they know you and you have no reason to assume that they will

react badly to being kissed by you. There are still times when you shouldn't kiss them: when they're eating a mouthful of food; when they are playing the French Horn in the school orchestra, particularly in the middle of a school concert; when they are giving mouth-to-mouth resuscitation to an accident victim, unless you are absolutely certain that the victim is beyond help and only after calling a doctor (or a vet, depending on the victim); when they are riding pillion on your motorbike; and especially if they have just been licking a hospital wall to see if the paint tastes of Avocado Pear.

The best times to kiss someone, who wants to be kissed, is in the comfort of a dark cinema, or at the romantic corner table of that special restaurant, or at home in front of the TV (but not in front of the relatives, and certainly not in front of a younger brother or sister, because you will never hear the last of it). The best place to kiss someone is anywhere where such a private moment can remain private, especially if there's a chance that you might blow it! (**SEE ALSO: HOBBIES, SELF DEFENCE**)

KYLIE MINOGUE'S HAIRDRESSER: HOW TO BECOME

(Keyelee-Min-OG-Yooz Hare-dress-a: Howe-2b-cum): This is easy. After all, she never stands still long enough to have her hair styled, let alone for anyone to see how well (or badly) it's been done. The easiest way to get the job is to write to her. Write to: Ms Kylie Minogue, Ramsey Street, Erinsborough, Australia, and say: "Dear Kylie, I thought you were dead good in *Neighbours*. Can I be your hairdresser, please?" That should do the trick. You could include something that proves that you are a serious hair stylist, like a photograph of your scissors. But I should think that she'd be only too glad to hear from you. After all, much more experienced stylists than you have probably tried to do something with Kylie's hair, and obviously failed. (**SEE ALSO: JASON DONOVAN, AUSTRALIAN**)

L

LANGUAGE: BODY *(Lang-Widg Bodd-ee):* Body Language is a fairly new thing. That is to say, we have always done it, but it is only quite recently that someone (probably an American) hit on the idea of making huge sums of money writing about it. So what is it? In simple terms, it is the shapes we make with our bodies – the way we hold our hands, cross our legs, arms, eyes and even teeth. These gestures apparently speak volumes about what we are actually thinking, without uttering a sound. Clever, eh? Obviously there is not room here to explain the entire science (anyway, someone else has already done that in a much thicker, more expensive book), but I can give you a few pointers. For example, if a person crosses their legs towards you, this means that they like you. If you put your hand on their knee, this means that you

He likes her

She likes him

He's gone too far

like *them*. If they then slap your face, this means that they don't like you *that* much! If you are talking to someone, and you find yourself waving your hands about a lot, this probably means that you are subconsciously trying to keep their attention. If they suddenly lie perfectly still on the floor, this probably means that you have failed. Although I suppose that it could mean that you've accidentally breathed on them. (**SEE ALSO: BAD BREATH**) But you see how it works? It's very clever, so long as you can follow it. Of course, if you are confused by it, no doubt the other person will eventually explain what they are trying to say. (**SEE ALSO: BUNCH OF FIVES, HOSPITAL FOOD**).

LAWYER: JOB OPPORTUNITY *(Lor-yer: Gob-opper Tune-Itty):* Not the best of jobs, as it does involve work. It is similar to the job of Barrister, without the added fun of the dressing up. He does, however, get briefs – unlike a solicitor, who can represent you, whether he's wearing briefs or not. I have referred to the lawyer throughout as *He*, because the Law does tend to be a male stronghold, although more and more women are being called to the Bar (as Barristers and Lawyers, not barmaids). This is regarded by many in legal circles as a bad thing, which is probably one of the reasons why they say: "The Law is an Ass." (**SEE ALSO: GETTING A JOB, BARRISTER, DOCTOR, SPEAKER – HOUSE OF COMMONS**)

LEARNING AN INSTRUMENT *(Ler-Ningan-inst-rummant):* Having selected your instrument, explore it. Get to know it. Personally I think that musical instruments should be marked: Easy, Fairly Easy, Harder, Waste Of Money If You're Tone Deaf, etc. This would save so much time and energy. If your chosen instrument is the guitar, you will probably need a book to show you how to hold it, form chord shapes, etc. Although if you have a slow button on your video machine, you can video *Top of the Pops*, play it back frame by frame, and pick up the handling and chord shapes from there. A word of warning: pick a band who look as though they know what

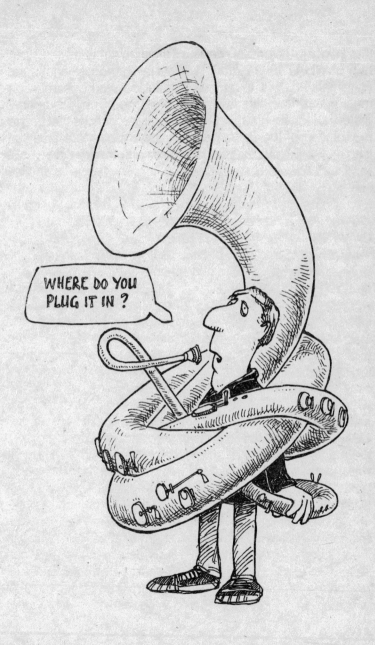

they're doing. (**SEE ALSO: FORMING A BAND**)

LOVE: WHAT IS IT? *(Luv: Wotizzit?):* I'm honestly not sure. Apparently it's the thing that makes the world go round. I must admit that, although my knowledge of physics is very limited, I had thought that the inter-stellar reactions that cause the rotation of the Earth were probably a bit more complex than that. Still, you never can tell! (**SEE ALSO: ACTS OF GOD**)

M

M25: *(Em-Twen-Tee-Five):* For some time now, people have been very worried about the number of cars on our roads. One reason for the worry is the damage that leaded petrol is doing to our atmosphere. There are other reasons, too, of course: lack of parking space, traffic accidents, wear and tear on the roads, etc. People have been urging the Government for years to do something about it, but the Government *seem* not to care. Is this because of the fact that reduction in car sales would affect our economy? No, it can't be that, because everyone drives a foreign car anyway. In fact, not many people realize this, but the Government have already set a plan in motion which they hope will solve the problem. The code name for this plan is M25. This is how they hope the plan will work: They have built a motorway, which is a complete circle, going all the way around London (the capital city). People have been led to believe that this road will save them a great deal of time, because it avoids London and all the major towns in the south of England. Encouraged by this, motorists drive on to the M25. But they never get off again. They just go round and round in circles. There are no services, so they can't stop for food, petrol, or a pee. They just have to keep going and going, until they or their car gives up the ghost. It's a sort of Bermuda Triangle. Every now and again the road is closed (they call this Road Works), so that the debris can be cleared. Brilliant, isn't it? Let's hope that the motorists never catch on and stop using the M25. So, keep it to yourself!

MAGAZINES *(Mag-az-eenz):* With reading becoming more and more popular, even though people are becoming less and less good at it, the Magazine market has been flooded. There is now a magazine to cover every possible pleasure, pastime, sport or hobby. Except Bear Baiting. And Mole Strangling. And Public Hanging. Well, there probably is, but I haven't seen them. But why are there so many magazines?

Who knows! But what actually sells a magazine is not the quality of the contents, but the free gifts. Let's face it, a mag about computers with a free floppy-disc stuck on the front is bound to be more popular than one that is just stuffed with lots of computer-friendly jargon. I wonder how long it will be before Hi-Fi Mags have a free CD stuck on the front, or a Mag about Steeplechasing has a horse stuck on the front. I pity the poor paper kid when that happens. How are they going to get it through the letter box? But, if these mags have got different free gifts stuck on the front, what have they got inside? The same stuff, really: interviews, features (which is another word for interviews), articles (which is another word for features), readers' letters. What sort of people write to magazines? Train spotters, probably:

> Dear Jugglers Weekly,
>
> I know that you normally only print letters from people with some form of sexual disorder, but I thought that your readers might be interested to know that yesterday I spotted a DL 89765Z2 pulling a Series 7 Bogie Bolster, which I think you'll agree is pretty unusual in anybody's language.
>
> Yours sincerely,
> Excited of Wigan

Magazines tend to have names that tell you exactly what they're about:
Girl: A mag for girls.
Jackie: A mag for girls who are called Jackie. (How sexist! Why isn't there a mag called *Colin*?)
Pigeon Fancier's Weekly: A mag for people who fancy pigeons once a week.
This is very helpful, as it means that

you don't have to bother to read them! (**SEE ALSO: RIP-OFFS**)

MAKING YOUR OWN CLOTHES *(May King yorone cloze):*
This is not as difficult as you might imagine, if indeed you were imagining that it *was* difficult. All you need is some materials, and a body. Your own body will do, as the clothes are for you. The materials can be anything. For instance, there's a bit of a 1970s revival at the moment (there's been one struggling along for years!), and Plastic Bin Liners make great Wet Look garments. Old curtains, or even wallpaper, make great flowered shirts/blouses. Of course, the great advantage to making clothes for yourself is that you don't need to sew them. You can stick them straight to your body. Obviously, bear in mind when you do this that you might want to take them off if they go out of fashion, or when you become a High Court Judge. So it's as well to avoid using Superglue. Of course, there will be those people whose fashion sense is entirely dictated by the great fashion houses, and they might turn their nose up at your efforts (particularly if your clothes are stuck on with very smelly wallpaper paste). But just because your clothes are homemade, it doesn't mean that they are any less trendy than the most expensive "Designer" label. However, if you move in the sort of circles where designer labels are important, all you need to do is buy yourself a few designer garments, cut the labels off and stick them on your own creations. Your friends will be amazed! (**SEE ALSO: FASHION, FASHION SLAVE, RIP-OFFS**)

MAKING YOUR OWN SATELLITE DISH *(May-King yorone Sat-alight Dish):* The time may come, although I appreciate that you'll probably find this hard to believe, but the time may come when possessing a satellite dish will be regarded as something of a status symbol. And when this time comes, you won't want to be left behind, will you? Of course, persuading your parents to cough up for a dish may be tricky, but there really is no need. You can make your own!

You *can*. It's easy, I will tell you how. All you need is a dustbin lid, some bits of piping (an old bike frame will do) and some other bits of old rubbish. Then follow these simple instructions:

MAKE YOUR OWN
~ SATELLITE DISH ~

fig I TAKE A DUSTBIN LID, BIT OF BIKE, HAMMER AND NAILS, AND STRING.

fig II NAIL LID TO SIDE OF HOUSE...

TINKLE TINKLE

SMASH

CRACK!

WRONG

RIGHT

fig III ATTACH BIT OF BIKE WITH STRING.

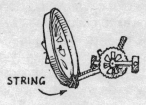

STRING

There! I told you it was easy, didn't I? But you may be thinking, "How am I going to receive TV programmes on an old dustbin lid? Surely I need a scrambler and all that stuff, don't I?" Yes. You do. But I never said anything about *receiving* programmes, did I? All you need is the dish. Your friends don't need to know that you can't actually pick up the programmes, do they? Just as long as you don't get flash and invite them round to watch. Nor, in fact, do you need to see the programmes in order to be able to talk about them. You just need to be old, or know someone who's old. Because most of the TV programmes have been on before, many years ago. As for the new programmes, well if anyone asks you "What did you think of *Name that Washing* last night?", just reply: "Rubbish!"; you're bound to be right! (**SEE ALSO: GAME SHOWS, TV PRESENTERS (CHILDREN'S)**

MIKE SMITH: CONDITION *(Myk-Smith: Con-Dishun):* A burning desire to be Noel Edmunds. This condition is also known as Lack of Ambition. (**SEE ALSO: SARAH GREEN, BRANDRETH, RANTZEN, JEFFREY ARCHER**)

MUSO: DEFINITION *(Mewzo: deaf-In-Ishun):* This is an expression that you might hear musicians use. It means, surprisingly enough, Musician. Now, there is a very good reason why musicians favour this term: it's short. Musicians, you see, have great trouble with words of more than one syllable. Oh, they can play the whole of *Stairway to Heaven* or *Rachmaninov's Symphony No 2 in E Minor Opus 27* without drawing breath, but get them to attempt to say something like "The Leith Police Dismisseth Us", and they'll require major jaw surgery before the end of the first word. (**SEE ALSO: FORMING A BAND, TOURING WITH YOUR BAND/GROUP, NAMING YOUR BAND**)

MUZ BIZ: DEFINITION *(Muz-Biz: Deaf-In-Ishun):* This is one of those trendy phrases people use when they mean the Music Business. It's the kind of term used by Posers who have absolutely nothing to do with the music industry, such as

TV Presenters, TV Researchers, etc. Not the sort of term you should use if you want to impress anyone who knows anything about music, but great if you just want to show off to a few first-years! (**SEE ALSO: FORMING A BAND, TOURING WITH YOUR BAND/GROUP**)

N

NAMING YOUR BAND *(Nay-Ming Yor Banned):* Having got your band together (**SEE: FORMING A BAND**) you need to think of a name for it. The main thing to bear in mind is that the name needs to be something that DJs can say, which of course does limit your choice rather. You could go for something very simple and straightforward that tells your audience as much about your band as possible. For example: The Kenny Ball Jazz Band. That tells you quite a lot. It tells you that the band is a jazz band, and that it's got someone called Kenny Ball in it. It doesn't, unfortunately, tell you that listening to them is like having your toe-nails removed without the aid of a local anaesthetic (or even an anaesthetic from a nearby town). You could, on the other hand, pick a name that suggests you're something you're not. Such as Spandau Ballet, who are not a ballet. Or something totally meaningless, like Duran Duran, who aren't either. Then there's the idea of naming the band after the musicians in it, such as Dave Dee, Dozy, Beaky, Mick and Titch, who were very big in the sixties, or Simon and Garfunkel, who have never been particularly tall. This method of naming a band was very popular in the sixties. For example: Emerson, Lake and Palmer had a line-up that consisted of Keith Emerson (keyboards), Greg Lake (drums) and Arnold Palmer (golf clubs). The only problem there is if band members leave, you'll have to keep changing the name of the band. For instance: Crosbie, Stills, Nash and Young. Originally they were called Crosbie, Stills; then Neil Young joined them and they became Crosbie, Stills and Young. Then Graham Nash joined them, and they became Crosbie, Stills, Nash and Young, then Neil Young left and they became Crosbie Stills and Nash. In fact, I believe they made the big mistake of changing the band's name every time one of them went to the toilet.

Of course, it's quite popular these days to name the band after some of the equipment. For instance: We've Got A Fuzzbox, who have got a fuzzbox, and Echo and The Bunnymen, who have got a rabbit. But if this is the route you decide to go don't make the mistake of being too literal. So, for example, calling your band We've Got A Synth Two Guitars Drums And Sax Oh And Kev's Got A Mouth Organ But He Keeps Forgetting To Bring It isn't going to impress anybody, except Kev's Mum.

The other important thing to remember when picking your band's name, is to suit the name to the type of music you play. For instance: Devil's Axemen or The Turbo-Throbbers would be quite good names for a heavy metal band, whereas The Raving Harlots would be quite a bad name for a Gospel Group. It's also important to pick a name that encourages people to want to see you. For this reason Taxman, The Dentists, or The School Dinnerladies would be bad names to pick.

One final tip: having picked your name, make sure you're spelling it correctly – unlike Then Jerico. This is almost as important as not calling yourselves The Something Five when there are seven of you. Incidentally, calling yourself The Three Somethings or The Something Five can have repercussions when you're touring. (**SEE ALSO: TOURING WITH YOUR BAND/GROUP, POP FAME, LEARNING AN INSTRUMENT**)

NURSING: JOB OPPORTUNITY *(Ner-sing: Gob-opper Tune-Itty):* Many people, when they are about to leave school, decide that they want to do something useful with their life, to *serve* humankind. Many of these people get their wish and end up working in shops, but some decide to become nurses. Traditionally this has been a female occupation, but more and more men are being attracted to it. It's probably the uniform. But what *is* nursing? Well, it's a bit like doctoring, really, without the kudos. A nurse looks after the patient, cleans them up, and makes them presentable for when the doctor comes visiting. After all, doctors can't be expected to diagnose someone if all their pyjama buttons aren't done up!

The difference between doctors and nurses is that nurses are very badly paid. Mind you, they work such long hours that they wouldn't have time to spend the extra money, even if they were given it. But why are nurses so badly paid? Well, there's a very good reason for that – probably. Still, nursing is a *calling*, isn't it? Or, so we keep being told. And, in common with most *callings*, it doesn't pay enough to live on. But, as the Nurse goes about his or her daily task of caring for the sick, and trying to make ends meet, they can fall asleep on duty, safe in the knowledge that, not only are they saving lives, but they're also saving the Health Service money. (**SEE ALSO: DOCTOR, DENTIST, RECEPTIONIST**)

O

OPTICIAN *(Op-tishun):* "Men don't make passes at girls who wear glasses." I don't know who said this originally, but it can't be true, because glasses are probably more popular now than they've ever been. There used to be some sort of stigma attached to wearing glasses. The kids in specs were always among the last six when it came to that humiliating experience – picking teams. Foureyes was always regarded as a Swot, which is stupid, because you don't have to be intelligent to have bad eyesight. I wear glasses, so that proves it! But, what a life being an Optician! Spending all day encouraging people to read a card, while secretly hoping that they won't be able to, so that they can sell them an over-priced pair of spectacles? Actually, Opticians must be really fed up, because you can buy glasses virtually anywhere these days: "Two pounds of best quality mince and a pair of bi-focals, please Butcher!" Where will it end? I pity the poor Opticians. After all, they're only trying to make a living. Perhaps *they* should branch out a bit – start taking in washing or something. (**SEE ALSO: GETTING A JOB, RECEPTIONIST, NURSING, CONTACT LENSES**)

OZONE LAYER: WHAT IS IT? *(O-Zone-Lay-er: Wotizzit?):* In common with more or less everyone else in the world, I have little or no idea. All I know is that it's got a hole in it, and that we should be worried about it. I can understand that. I worry about things getting holes in them. Mostly socks. But normally I put it down to built-in obsolescence. Perhaps that's what the hole in the ozone layer is – built-in obsolescence. God made Heaven and Earth, etc. in six days. On the seventh day He rested. But perhaps not. Perhaps He spent the seventh giving the Earth built-in obsolescence. I think it's very unlikely, but next time I see a Jehovah's Witness, I'll ask him to find out. (**SEE ALSO: ACTS OF GOD, BUILT-IN OBSOLESCENCE, JEHOVAH'S WITNESSES, GREENHOUSE EFFECT**)

P

PARENTS *(Pear-antz):* It is common for these to come in pairs, although it is quite easy to mislay one, or both, along the way. After all, life's journey is a bumpy one, and there have been cases of parents (well, not actually *cases*. Parents don't come in cases, or even boxes) who have fallen off the backs of lorries. They are very similar to an old familiar blanket that you know you've outgrown, but can't throw away, somehow. They always seem to know what's best for you, while making a total muddle of their own lives. They can interfere so much that they drive you to drink. This usually happens shortly after they stop driving you to school. (Read also: *Coping With Parents*, written by me and published by HIPPO!)

PARTIES: THROWING YOUR OWN *(Par-Teas: Thro-ing yorone):* Parties can be great, but you do need to lay down a few ground rules first. You'd also be advised to lay down a few ground-*sheets* as well! Because parties can get very messy. I'm not entirely sure why, but it does seem to be one of those strange-but-true facts of life, that when you're really enjoying yourself, food and drink tend to miss your mouth. Maybe this is how you tell that you're having a good time: "Wow! I must really be Getting It On, I'm knee-deep in vegetarian quiche!" A bit of mess can be tolerated, as long as you can get it cleaned up afterwards. But because everyone suddenly disappears at the mention of tidying up (even the ones who are unconscious), it's best to secure promises of help *before* the party starts. Basically you'll need a couple of girls who everyone thinks would make good wives, which is usually a polite way of saying that they're plain and boring. Failing this, find a couple of boys who everyone thinks would make good wives. Oh, and you'll also need a tall person for scraping stuff off the ceiling. If you're really clever, however, you may be able to incorporate the cleaning into the party, by suggesting a game of Hunt The Dropped Food, offering a prize for the person who collects up the most. An extension to this would be Hunt And Eat The Dropped Food; that way you solve the problem of disposing of it as well. This will only work, though, on people who are more stupid than you are, so be careful!

Here are a few handy hints that might help your party run smoothly:

(1) *Parents*: Make sure that they are well out of the way. Locking them in a cupboard will not work. Neither will allowing them to stay in the other room. They'll either keep spying and turning down the music, or they'll want to join in. There's nothing more embarrassing than a Dad who suddenly appears in flares, carrying an armful of old 78's, and saying: "Come on! Let's have some *real* music!" No.

It's best to suggest that they go somewhere for the evening, like Barbados.

(2) *Trouble*: This comes in many forms, from the person who throws up, to the person who gate-crashes. There's not an awful lot you can do about gate-crashers, apart from employing a Private Security firm. You could, I suppose, post your Dad on the door, but then no one would get in, except possibly a couple of Jehovah's Witnesses. However you can do something about the Party Chuck-Upper. Check around your friends, and find out who threw up at *their* party. It's bound to be the same person at yours. There are those people whose role in life is to be a Party Chuck-Upper, just as there are those who are destined to be Chuck-Upees (ie: the person who gets thrown up over). There are also the Clearer-Uppers, the Consolers, and the I'll-Phone-Your-Dadders (Not to mention the guy who says, "I'll take her outside for some fresh air", and then tries to get off with her!) So, try to find out roughly what time the Chuck-Upper usually does their party-piece (you can set your watch by them as a rule), and have a Clearer-Upper standing by with a bucket. If properly organized, it needn't even stop the dancing. In my experience, people hardly ever notice, anyway. It's only when they do it in the punch that it gets anti-social.

(3) *Bonking*: There's really not much you can do about this. If you lock all the bedrooms and electrify the back lawn, you'll still find them in the airing cupboard. It's best just to make sure that they don't crease the coats, or frighten the family pet.

(4) *Alcohol*: Parents will usually have laid down fairly strict rules about this. As you may know, it is not essential to be drunk in order to have a good time. In fact, if you want to *remember* having a good time, it's obligatory to stay sober. But not everyone knows this. However, they aren't

difficult to spot. They're the ones who bring a 99p bottle of Low-Alcohol Cider, two cans of Italian lager, or a bottle they've pinched from home (usually oven-cleaner). You know very well that they're not going to drink it, they're going to make straight for your Mum's cooking sherry. All you can do is keep an eye on things. The ones to watch are those who only ever drink at parties. They're often found in the kitchen, near the sink (which is fortunate, really!)

(5) *Smoking*: Again its best to lay down rules, particularly if your parents are non-smokers, or value their carpet. Obviously you don't want to spoil people's fun, but I don't think anyone could consider you unreasonable if you said: "I don't mind anyone smoking, but if you set fire to the house, I might have to ask you to leave."

(6) *Staying the Night*: Obviously there will be people who want to stay the night, either because they live too far away and can't get home, or because they've got stuck in the airing cupboard. Most parents are quite happy about this (the staying over, I mean, not the airing cupboard!). Of course, it's an added bonus if you can get non-smokers, non-drinkers, non-bonkers and keen cleaner-uppers to stay over. This is very rare, though, since most of them go home at nine! (SEE ALSO: PARENTS, DRINK AND DRUGS)

PARTIES: THROWING UP AT YOUR OWN *(Par-teas: thro-ing upatt yorone):* It is strangely far less acceptable to throw up at your own party than it is to throw up at someone else's. I suppose that if it's someone else's, everyone assumes that you're having a great time, but if it's your own, they assume that you're dropping subtle hints to try and get them all to leave! (SEE ALSO: DRINK AND DRUGS, DISCOS)

PEER PRESSURE *(Pee-er Presher):* Peer Pressure does not refer to Members of the House of Lords making you do things (although it could, if *you* were a Peer yourself). It refers to pressure put on you by your "peer group", people of the same age and status as you – your friends, mates at school, etc. So what kind of pressure do they put on you? I'm not talking about bullying here. I'm talking about your feeling that you should behave in a certain way or dress in a certain way because your pals do. Very often peer pressure is completely unspoken, but it's every bit as powerful as bullying. Imagine the situation: You are out on the town with a gang of mates, and a couple of them decide to do something that on the face of it is wrong, but not exactly *criminal*. They might be boys just doing it to impress the girls in the group, or girls trying to impress the boys. But they need the help of the rest of you. Some of the rest of the group are keen, but you're not too sure. What do you do? Say, "Not me. We might get caught", and risk being called Chicken or Wally or whatever? Or do you go along with the majority, telling yourself that, after all, it's not a bad thing that you're doing, and who's going to know, if you don't get caught? It is probably as well at times like this to remember that you are an individual, and some day you will move into a different peer group. And the only things you might take with you from this present peer group are a few happy memories, and a criminal record.

PLUGGERS *(pluggerz):* Record companies employ people called Pluggers. It is the Plugger's job to get records played on the radio, videos shown on TV, etc. If you form a band and make a record, then this person could be your lifeline. It would depress you, then, if you met one, since you would realize what little chance you had of success with them as your only hope! So, how does plugging work? Well, basically the Plugger contacts the radio/TV station (by phone or in person), and asks them to play the record. They may have a small number of records to plug at any given time, so an ability to tell these records apart is a useful quality for a Plugger. Musical ability is not a prerequisite. In fact it can be a disadvantage, as there are as many bad records made each week as there are good ones, and the Plugger has to try and shift them all. In the past there have been accusations of bribery levelled at Pluggers, but I think all that is a thing of the past. All they usually need to do is say: "Unless you play this record, I'll make you listen to it!" (SEE ALSO: MUZ BIZ, MUSO)

PLUKES *(Plookz):* See Zits. Basically I believe that a Pluke is a Scottish Zit. This is obviously something that Shakespeare didn't realize when he wrote: "Out! Out! Damn'd spot!" (Macbeth Act V scene 1). (SEE ALSO: ZITS, SPOTS, ACNE)

POCKET CALCULATOR *(Pok-It Cal-Cewl-Ater):* Basically it's the brain in your pocket. A quick way of solving a problem. As long as the problem is mathematical, and you know how to use the calculator. And, more importantly, have a basic knowledge of maths in the first place. When calculators were first introduced into schools, this simple truth was overlooked. Which meant that some pupils' mathematical ability was entirely dependent on how good the batteries were in their calculator. Because, whatever answer their calculator gave them, they knew no better than to believe it: "1 plus 1? Seven billion and forty-six? Thank you very much!" Still – that's progress! (SEE ALSO: SCHOOL: AVOIDING, ACCOUNTANT)

POLICE *(Pleees):* We live in an increasingly violent society, and the role of the average Policeman has become an increasingly more difficult one. And yet everyone seems to think that they can poke fun at the Police. This book is no exception:

> *Person A:* How many policemen does it take to change a light bulb?
>
> *Person B:* Is that with or without an instruction book?

(SEE ALSO: ACID HOUSE PARTIES, ROTTWEILERS, DISCOS, FOOT-BALL)

POLITICIAN: JOB OPPORTUNITY *(Polly Tishun: Gob-opper Tune-Itty):* One of those great jobs that require no real qualifications. A job that really suits anyone who doesn't like working, but doesn't mind talking. In fact, you don't even have to talk, if you don't want to. Even if you do, everything you say will be taken down and misquoted in the Press, so why bother? (SEE ALSO: SUN) I suppose, since they've started televising Parliament, it might be as well to throw in the odd word now and then, but a good loud "Hear! Hear!" will be enough. The only real drawback is that you will have to visit your constituents occasionally. But, after all, they do vote for you, so it's the least you can do. Of course, this can be a drag, as very often these people live Up North, have funny accents, and are really not your sort at all. But it's only two or three times a year, and at election time. Once you've been re-elected, you can move as far away from them as possible. Hampshire's very nice. (SEE ALSO: GETTING A JOB, SPEAKER – HOUSE OF COMMONS)

POP FAME *(Popp-phaym):* Some musicians are lucky enough to become famous. If they are *really* lucky, they get to become famous before they've spent hundreds of hours learning to play their instruments. But, before you start saying to yourself: "Cor! That sounds OK! I think I'll become a famous pop star!", I should point out that many many bands never become famous at all. And many of the bands that do are only famous for a very short time. It's usually about four weeks. Of course, with careful planning you could arrange for your band to be famous for four weeks around the end of June and the beginning of July. That way you could go on holiday in August without getting hassled, because by then no one will remember who you were! (SEE ALSO: FORMING A BAND)

POSERS *(Po-Zerz):* We all know them. They've got all the latest designer labels (sewn on to BHS clothes). They can talk with authority about the latest dances, the latest CDs, the latest trends. They make up the audience of C4's *Club X*, but would not be seen dead on *Top of the Pops*. They are the envy of everyone, until you talk to them (or, God forbid, go out with them). And then you realize why they spend so much time on their Image. It's because it's all they've got! They are not exactly thick, but never top of the class. So they'll never make a micro-surgeon, even though they'd look brilliant in the white coat. They tend to gravitate towards the professions where looks mean a great deal more than ability. The Media is full of them! (**SEE ALSO: DISCOS, IMPRESSING YOUR DATE**)

PUBERTY *(Pew-Burty):* Puberty is that difficult time of your life, around early to mid-teenage, when your voice gets deeper, hair starts to grow on your body and chin, and you have to start shaving twice a day. And that's just the girls. What makes this time doubly difficult is that you start getting really strong feelings about things. Like football and hockey. You suddenly want to play it professionally. Boys even stop wanting to be train drivers. Even the ones who eventually become train drivers. Girls start wanting to do things that they'd always thought were soppy. Like working in a hairdresser's. It's a difficult time. For some young people it gets so bad that they start fancying the opposite sex. But, don't worry, it wears off! (**SEE ALSO: DATES, IMPRESSING YOUR DATE, LOVE**)

PUNK: DEFINITION *(Punk: Deaf-in-Ishun):* Of all the music styles, Punk was possibly the most aggressive, alarming, and exciting. Pins through the nose, legs chained together, tattoos all over the face. I often wonder what would happen if one of those punks suddenly turned his back on the whole thing, went *straight*, and eventually became a High Court Judge. What would he do about the tattoos? Pull his wig down over his face? Still, Punks and High Court Judges do have a lot in common. They both involve extreme forms of dressing-up.

The major band of the Punk movement was the Sex Pistols, created by Malcolm McLaren. McLaren made a film about the Sex Pistols, entitled *The Great Rock and Roll Swindle*. I went to see this film, and was very intimidated by a large proportion of the audience, who were all shouting and being generally Punk. They were all decked out in Punk gear, and all had their legs chained together. The lights went down. The film came on. McLaren came on to the screen and explained that the whole punk thing had been a big rip-off to make money. The lights came up. The audience sat there in silence, looking very sheepish. They all now knew that they had been ripped-off. I was very glad that I wasn't a punk at that moment, otherwise I would have been looking down at my chained legs and wondering what the hell I thought I looked like, just as everyone else was! I also felt very glad that I was not the sort of person who says: "I told you so!" **(SEE ALSO: PEER PRESSURE, FASHION)**

105

Q

QUEEN: HM THE *(The Kween Aich-Em-the):* Not every country has a constitutional monarch. Mind you, not every country wants one. But we in England have, whether we want one or not. You see, you can't really do away with the monarchy without an Act of Parliament, and that Act would have to be signed by the Queen. And she's not going to do herself out of a job, is she? After all, she's no fool. How can she be? You don't become Queen by having the brain of a belt-loop, do you? Apart from being Queen, the Queen is

A royal party

Head of State, Head of the Church of England, Defender of the Faith, and hundreds of other things. She also throws some pretty good parties, so I've heard. She is also kept pretty busy opening things, like factories (which then get closed again), hospitals (ditto), and letters. She gets hundreds of letters. Naturally she doesn't reply to them all personally. She has Ladies in Waiting to do that. But she makes sure that they put, "The Queen has asked me to say . . .", as in:

Dear Melanie,
    The Queen has asked me to say thank you for sending her your pet gerbil, which she confirms is in fact dead. She does not feel that the Royal Doctor will be able to do much for it.
    Yours Sincerely,
Lady Felicity Stain-Remover,
Lady in Waiting to the Royal Bed-Pan

Royalty has a massive staff, all of whom have strange titles, such as Fellow of the Bedchamber, Keeper of the Royal Dog Biscuits, etc, and all of whom would be out of a job if we didn't have a Monarch. Where else would they get employed in their chosen profession? There isn't a great deal of call for Keepers of Royal Dog Biscuits, is there?

QUIET: WHAT IS IT? *(Kweye-ert: Wotizzit?):* Quiet is that unusual state when there is no sound, and no movement to make a sound. When you could hear a pin drop, although one wouldn't be dropped, because that would destroy the state of quiet. It's a thing that Adults are very keen on, not realizing that they would get it all the sooner if they stopped yelling about it, since it is their voice alone that is preventing Quiet being achieved. There is a feeling among some Adults that Young People are incapable of Quiet. This is, of course, not true. It's just that they are less obsessed with it than their older counterparts. Some teachers seem to believe that you

R

RADIO ONE *(Raid-Ee-O Won):* Britain's favourite radio, according to the BBC. Something that always amazes me is the fact that the disc jockeys never look like their voices (they're all far too big to be jockeys too). They don't, do they?

The Radio One DJs in particular all look like School Prefects. Especially Steve Wright. Simon Bates looks very pompous, but maybe that's not so surprising. Mike Read looks like Cliff Richard, only about 70 years younger. That's probably because Mike Read *is* 70 years younger. Gary Davis looks like Dr Jekyll – *after* he's drunk the potion! Those are never his own eyebrows, are they? But it is odd that none of them sound like their voices. Perhaps they don't *do* the voices. Perhaps the voices are done by people so frighteningly ugly that they cannot appear in the flesh. So the BBC, realizing that

Steve Wright in the afternoon

Steve Wright at any other time of day

these Uglies would have to appear on *Top of the Pops*, thought that they'd better replace them in public with really good-looking people. Mind you, if that is the case, why haven't they done it? (**SEE ALSO: DISCOS, POSERS, PUNK**)

RANTZEN: CONDITION *(Ran-San: Con-Dish-un):* Although this sounds like a Chinese dish, it isn't either Chinese or a dish. It is a condition. One that lasts seemingly for ever, and affects the sense of humour in serious ways. Sufferers find themselves taking an almost unnatural interest in rudely-shaped vegetables (usually carrots). Advanced forms of this condition can involve the sufferer being unable to complete a sentence themselves, but having to employ large numbers of young men to complete the sentences for them. Unless checked, this condition can develop into a state of collecting newspaper clippings that contain double meanings. Specialist help should be sought when the sufferer starts going out on to the street, dressed as an old woman (ie: not wearing any make-up), and accosting members of the public. The condition can only really be controlled by involving the sufferer in some serious and worthwhile project, such as Childline where they immediately flourish, and become useful members of society once more. (**SEE ALSO: BRANDRETH, RUSSELL GRANT**)

REALLY COOKING!: EXPRESSION *(Reel-Ee Cuk-In!: X-Presh-un):* An expression used to demonstrate a certain amount of excitement, as in: "Now we're really cooking!" It basically means that your dinner's nearly ready.

RECEPTIONIST: JOB OPPORTUNITY *(Resep-shunist: Gob-opper Tune-Itty):* This is a great job if you can be all things to all people. This is partly because the types of Receptionist job are many and varied, but also because the duties of a Receptionist are also infinite. Take the Doctor's Receptionist, for instance. You need to be able to be gentle and sympathetic to the patient who comes into the surgery, offhand and callous to the patient who phones up for a home visit. This is because Doctors are overworked, and home visits really take up a lot of time. The Australians have the right idea, with their Flying Doctor service (SEE ALSO: AUSTRALIAN) A good line to put off the patient requiring a home visit would be: I'm sorry, but Dr Turnip is only visiting the Clinically dead this morning." Or: "Is it serious?", with an air of *you don't sound ill to me!* Another popular one, used regularly by our local Receptionist, is: "Why didn't you telephone earlier?" This is used irrespective of your problem:

> *You:* Hallo, is that the Doctor's surgery? I've just this very second chopped my leg off. Could a Doctor come out please?
> *Receptionist:* Why didn't you phone earlier?

It helps you to become a Doctor's Receptionist if you are a real Know-All. This enables you to do diagnoses over the phone, which can cut the Doctor's workload quite considerably, and some Receptionists are actually better at it than the Doctor. In fact, knowing everyone's business is the perfect quality for a Receptionist, whether working for a Doctor, a Dentist or in Big Business. It enables you to predict problems before they happen, and gives you something to bargain with if you're threatened with the sack! (SEE ALSO: TELEPHONIST, DOCTOR, DENTIST, GETTING A JOB, JOiNED-UP WRITING)

REG DWIGHT *(Redge-Dwite):* The real name of Elton John. It's enough to make your hair fall out, isn't it? No wonder he changed it! (SEE ALSO: NAMING YOUR BAND, POP FAME)

REGGAE: DEFINITION *(Regg-Ay: Deaf-in-Ishun):* Personally one of my favourite types of music. But it makes you walk in a funny way. You can always tell if someone is listening to reggae on their Walkman, because they are moving fairly slowly, with their legs bent, and their bum in a slight sitting position. They look almost as though they might have some

111

painful medical condition, affecting their bottom area (what some old people call the Undercarriage). Either that or they are smuggling lead in their underpants. Perhaps listening to reggae turns you into a lead smuggler! I think it's unlikely, but I think we should be told. **(SEE ALSO: DISCOS, MUZ BIZ, WALKMAN)**

REPORTS – SCHOOL *(Rep-ortz – Skule):* All schools are obliged from time to time to send reports home to your parents. This is partly to let your parents know how you're getting on at school, but also to prove that the teacher knows your name and address. Of course there have been cases of the wrong report going to the wrong house. What usually

happens in this case is that your Parents are delighted to hear that you are progressing well and are definitely university material, even though you seem to have changed your name, for some strange reason, to Nigel Dufflebag. But, they can't have everything, can they? Of course, it requires a fairly extensive education in the first place to understand the Report. Some Education Authorities are thinking of introducing Evening Classes to help parents understand these reports, which will probably become more frequent when the new school curriculum gets under way. Here is a rough guide to a few of the statements that teachers make about you:

Could do better: Can almost spell her own name.
Shows initiative: Cheats.
Vivid imagination: He must be on something!
Prefers to work unsupervised: Plays truant.
Mature, outgoing personality: Popular behind the bikesheds.
Makes a real effort: But still thick!
Comes alive in woodwork: Keeps sniffing the glue.
Prefers his own company: Stinks.
(SEE ALSO: SCHOOL: POINT OF, SCHOOL: AVOIDING, PARENTS)

RIP-OFFS *(Rip-ofz):* It is incredibly easy to get ripped off. After all, you bought this book, didn't you? But what exactly *is* a Rip-Off? Well, it's difficult to say, because it could be almost anything. But usually it turns out to be something that you regret buying, that you didn't really want in the first place but thought you did, and didn't realize until it was too late that you only thought you did want it, but you didn't really. Confused? That's the idea! That is how you get ripped-off! High powered advertising can probably persuade most people to buy most things. It's what they *don't* tell you that matters. A particular trendy new Stereo Stacking system has got the Lot: CD, digital thingy, dolby whatsisname, twin doodars, the lot! And it looks The Business! And it won't cost you the earth (**SEE ALSO: CREDIT**). It's compact, will look great in the corner of the room, won't gather dust, in fact the only thing it won't do is make the tea. Oh, and play records:

> *Shop assistant*: Well, sir, you never said anything about wanting to play records on it, did you?
> *You:* What did you think I was going to do with it? Doctor the cat?
> *Shop assistant*: Oh, I don't think it'll do that. But I can check in the manual, if sir would like to wait.
> *You*: "Sir" would rather have his money back.
> *Shop assistant:* Ah. That could be difficult. You see, it says in your agreement . . . just a minute, I'll fetch a magnifying glass.

AND SO IT GOES ON.

Of course, the chances are that you're too young to have entered into an HP agreement, so your Mum or Dad will feel obliged to fight on your side, as they will be ultimately responsible for seeing that you pay for it!

Of course, this is by no means the only kind of Rip-Off. Oh, no! There's the one where you buy something cheap, it falls apart as you take it out of the carrier bag, and you think, "Well, I got it so cheaply that I almost expected that to happen!", and so you hardly feel like complaining. Then of course there's the Record Industry Rip-Off. You buy a single, like it, and then discover that you can also get it in pink, or with a picture on it, in seven-inch, ten-inch or twelve-inch, CD or cassette, or get the same thing remixed, or remixed again, or a remix of the remix, which they also do in pink, or with a picture on it, in seven-inch, ten-inch or twelve-inch, CD or cassette. Then there's the Disco version . . . Not to mention the Instrumental version (that's the same thing with the vocals taken off). Then there's the sleeve. Or should I say sleeves, since they are available with different pictures of your Pop Idols on them. Oh! Have I mentioned the Mega-Mix? That's been so brilliantly mixed that it sounds exactly like the original single, except that it says Mega-Mix on the disc, so you know that it's different. And obviously that is available in all the colours and all the sizes. What is so special about the Mega-Mix is that they are pressing only a million copies. So you will be one of only a million people who own it. Think of that! That puts you in a fairly exclusive club, eh? Well, you and the other million people who bought it. Plus the million who bought it in pink, the million who bought it with a picture. The million who . . . are you getting the idea? And when the album comes out, all the singles are on it. Although, of course, they're not in pink, picture, seven-inch, etc. Not that you can tell that by listening to them, can you? **(SEE ALSO: CREDIT, BUILT-IN OBSOLESCENCE)**

ROTTWEILERS *(Rot-vile-erz):* Not so much a dog, more an

extension of the owner's personality. Except that Rottweilers, like their owners, tend not to have much personality beyond the instinct to kill. The Rottweiler is a perfect example of Man messing with nature. It is a dog that is specifically bred to be ferocious and violent, so that its owner can walk along and people can say: "Cor! There goes a ferocious and violent-looking dog. I bet that chap's very brave, owning a dog like that!" Unfortunately it doesn't always work out that way, as many passers-by think: "Well, that geezer looks a Complete Rodney, doesn't he? I bet he's got a brain the size of a paper-clip." Or, at least they would think that if the dog didn't eat them, halfway through their thinking it. But there are many examples of Man breeding and cross-breeding dogs in order to produce different breeds. For example, they've crossed an Irish Wolfhound with a Bulldog, to produce a dog that not only chases parked cars, but *looks* as though it does. (**SEE ALSO: KEEPING A PET, POSERS, SELF DEFENCE**)

RUBBERNECKS: WHAT ARE THEY? *(Rub-a-nex: Wot-R-thay?):* This is the term used to describe those people who make up the crowd around an accident. You get savaged half to death by a Rottweiler, you cry out piteously for help, and suddenly you find yourself surrounded. This restores your faith in human nature, until you realize that they are not there to help, they are there to *watch*. And to make matters worse, someone is bound to say, "Is the dog OK?", because Britain is a nation of dog lovers. We are not alone in this. There are other countries that love dogs, but they tend to love them boiled, fried or served with an orange sauce, not chasing after a ball, a person or a parked car. In many ways, traffic accidents are the worst kind, because they ruffle your clothing. In some cases they expose your underwear. In fact I think in all cases they expose your underwear. But, it is for precisely this reason that your Mum always insists that you go out of the house wearing clean stuff. And she's right! After all, I am inclined to believe that most Rubbernecks are only there for the Undies. After all, you can tell that they're not really thinking about the accident by the fact that they say things like: "Are you all right?" Of course you're not flipping well all right, for God's sake! You've just been run over! And to make matters much much worse, you're wearing yesterday's Undies! (**SEE ALSO: IMPRESSING YOUR DATE, LOVE, EATING OUT**)

RUSSELL GRANT: CONDITION *(Russle-Grant: Con-dish-n):* A condition that causes the sufferer to believe that all Pisceans are indecisive, all Cancerians are good with money, and all Librans have unsightly nasal hair. It also affects the voice and the weight, in that it causes both to go up and down. In severe cases it can lead to the wearing of ridiculous sweaters, and to the untrained eye can be mistaken for a bad case of Brandreth. The one consolation for the sufferer is that their mother will love them. (**SEE ALSO: BRANDRETH, RANTZEN**)

S

SAMPLING *(Sam Pling):* Currently very popular in the Muz Biz, sampling is the art of recording little bits from other people's records, mixing them together, and releasing them as your own. It has the added advantage over ordinary record making, that it doesn't really require any great musical skill. A good knowledge of the Muz Biz is obviously an advantage, as it enables you to pick records to sample that are by artists who are now dead, thus saving on royalty payments. And, naturally, once you've got the bits, you can keep rearranging them and releasing them as different discs. **(SEE ALSO: RIP-OFFS, MUZ BIZ, MUSO)**

SARAH GREEN: CONDITION *(Sair-ra Grene: Con-dish-n):* Not a particularly unpleasant condition, but a confusing one, since it gives the sufferer the impression that they are a TV Presenter, even though they know they can't be, since they have none of the requirements: they are not young, don't have a funny regional accent, and don't jump about and burble. The only requirement they have, in fact, is their ability to work with puppets – or is Philip Scofield actually human? The only drawback to this condition is that the sufferer tends to wind up getting married to Mike Smith. **(SEE ALSO: MIKE SMITH, TV PRESENTER (CHILDREN'S))**

SCHOOL: AVOIDING *(Skule: A-Void-in):* This may or may not be a good thing. It depends largely on your school. But if you decide that School is not for you, then you need to set your avoiding plan in action as soon as possible. Do not delay; after all, you don't attend school for much of your life, so if you delay too long you may find that you've left before you've started avoiding tactics. So, how do you avoid school? Not turning up is one way, but that can obviously backfire and get you into trouble with your parents, the authorities, etc. What you really need to do is to create an image for yourself which will make the teachers wish that you weren't there. And by this I do not mean cause trouble. This can also misfire. No. Be helpful, ask questions, offer to do things, and fetch things. Popping along to the staffroom to get the teacher's notes that she forgot, or running other little errands, such as notes to other teachers, bribes to the dinner ladies, etc, can get you out of lots of lessons, and not get you into trouble for skiving. Promote an image of yourself as Keen but thick. If you are already keen but thick, then obviously this will help, although you are unlikely to realize that this is what you are – because you *are* so keen (and thick!). For instance:

Teacher: Who can tell me the capital of China?
(Your hand goes up like lightning.)
You: (Hissed enthusiastically) Miss, miss!
(IF YOU COULD MANAGE TO DRIBBLE A BIT HERE, JUST TO SHOW HOW KEEN YOU ARE, THIS WILL HELP.)
Teacher: (To you) Yes, Jason?
You: Is it Mackerel, Miss?
Teacher: (Taken aback) You think that the capital of China is Mackerel, do you Jason?
You: (Very earnestly) Oooh, yes, Miss. I do. Yes.
(THERE WILL BE A PAUSE, WHILE THE TEACHER WONDERS WHY SHE SPENT THREE YEARS AT UNIVERSITY, FOLLOWED BY TWO YEARS AT TEACHER TRAINING COLLEGE. SHE WILL SHAKE HER HEAD. SHE MAY EVEN BANG IT GENTLY ON HER DESK.)
Teacher: (Slowly) Jason?
You: (Very eagerly) Yes, Miss?
Teacher: Would you like to pop over to the chemists for me, dear, and get them to make up something for a nervous breakdown. Tell them to take their time preparing it. You're in no hurry.

You: Certainly, Miss.
(YOU LEAVE THE ROOM. A NICE TOUCH AT THIS POINT WOULD BE TO WAIT OUTSIDE FOR ABOUT TEN MINUTES, THEN GO BACK INTO THE CLASS.)
You: Er . . .
Teacher: Yes, Jason?
You: What was it you wanted me to do again, Miss?

That should do the trick. I was milk monitor at infant school. It's amazing how long it can take to deliver the milk around the classrooms. If you do the job properly, that is. It was probably due to kids like me that Mrs Thatcher, as Minister of Education, abolished school milk. She was obviously on to the Scam!

Of course, I would not want to give you the impression that school is a waste of time. Far from it. But it really depends *which* school. Your future success is more likely to be assured if you can put "Eton" down on your CV, as opposed to "Abattoir Street Comprehensive", although this does depend on your not letting yourself down at the interview:

Potential Boss: I see you went to Eton. How did you get on there?
You: OK. But I spent most of my time there delivering the milk, and collecting up dinner money.

Of course, this avoiding-school business is all very well, but it would not be an advisable thing to do if you had plans to become a teacher yourself one day! **(SEE ALSO: TEACHERS)**
SCHOOL: POINT OF *(Skule: Poontov):* Like it or not, all of us have, at some point in our lives, to go to school. Even Shakespeare, considered by many to be the greatest ever playwright, had something to say about it. Probably. But then, he was very bright, and had something to say about most things. **(SEE ALSO: SHAKESPEARE)** But what about the rest of us?

Well, that's where school comes in. If you're very lucky, pay attention and don't eat the school dinners, you can come out of school at sixteen being able to use a calculator and do joined-up writing. This is basically all you need, as most jobs these days require you to sit in front of a huge, expensive piece of modern technology, marvel at its brilliance, and switch it off when it's time to

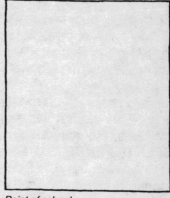

Point of school

go home. Oh, and get the sack if the machine decides to make a mistake. But at least such an all-round education means that you'll be able to read the paper, hold a simple conversation, and more-or-less follow the storyline of *Home and Away*. (**SEE ALSO: ACTS OF GOD, JOINED-UP WRITING, GETTING A JOB**)

SCHOOL DINNERS: WHAT ARE THEY? *(Skule Din-Erz: Wotarthay?):* No one knows. Not even the people who cook

PLEASE SIR, I DON'T WANT ANY MORE

them. It's like the mystery ingredient in Kentucky Fried Chicken. Nobody knows what that is. It certainly isn't chicken! School is full of mysteries. Like where does your homework go when the teacher loses it? Why are there lumps in the scum after school showers? Where does your Games Kit keep disappearing to? What happens to Teachers when they retire? Possibly these mysteries, plus the mystery about what school dinners are made of, are all linked in some strange way. (**SEE ALSO: SCHOOL: POINT OF, SCHOOL: AVOIDING**)

SELF DEFENCE *(Sell-f-dee-fence):* Originating in the East, in China and Japan, self defence (or Martial Arts) takes many forms: Judo, Kendo, Tai-Kwondo, Kung Fu, Karate, to name just a few. Although they have been around for centuries, they have become much more popular over the last twenty years through films and television series. For instance: *Karate Kid I* and *II*, the *Kung Fu* series with David Carradine, and the *Bruce Lee* films, with Bruce Lee. But what of the Arts themselves? Well, they are traditionally steeped in religion and eastern folk lore, involve a lifetime of self denial as you work your way through the various Dans and different-coloured belts. Then, and only then, are you ready for the supreme test – breaking a bit of wood. But if you make it, it will stand you in good stead. You will become a giant among men (and women). You won't even need to buy a Rottweiler. After all, would *you* tackle someone who could break a bit of wood? I certainly wouldn't! (**SEE ALSO: BUNCH OF FIVES, ROTTWEILERS**)

SHAKESPEARE: WHO WAS HE? *(Shakes-pee-er: Oowozzee?):* William Shakespeare was known as The Greatest Living Playwright until he died. Now he is known as the Greatest Dead Playwright. Born in Stratford-upon-Avon, a small town on the river Avon in what used to be called Warwickshire, but is now called Avon for some reason, he moved to London for the nightlife. Even in those days London had everything: rats, plague, the Great Fire, public hanging,

drawing and quartering (at Tyburn, which is now Marble Arch) – the lot. Shakespeare wrote over three dozen plays: the so-called "Histories" which took as their plots events from history, the "Tragedies", which were short on laughs, and the "Comedies", which were also short on laughs unless you liked jokes about identical twins and women dressed up as men. Shakespeare often appeared in his own plays, playing the parts that no one else wanted. He returned to Stratford and died – of boredom. A theatre was erected in his honour, and called the Royal Shakespeare Company. Since his death there has been some speculation as to whether he wrote the plays attributed to him, or not. There is a school of thought that believes that Francis Bacon wrote the plays. This is very very unlikely, but if it were ever proved to be true, then the Royal Shakespeare Company would have to be re-named: The Royal Bacon Company.

SNOOKER (*Snew-ker):* Part of the Great Plot to stop kids watching TV (**SEE ALSO: CRICKET, WIMBLEDON**). A passion for playing Snooker is usually a sign of a misspent youth, just as a passion for Fruit Machines is usually a sign of misspent pocket money. Snooker contains some very interesting Body Language. For instance, if a player stops to chalk his cue for several minutes, this usually means that he has no idea what he's doing, and will probably lose. However, in the case of Steve Davis, it usually means that he's trying to make himself look more interesting. Alex Higgins is probably using it to find out which end of the cue is which. (**SEE ALSO: BODY LANGUAGE, FAME, POSERS**)

SOAP: WHAT IS IT? *(Sope: Wotizzit?):* If you're wondering why someone keeps leaving the cheese on the bathroom sink, you've probably got something wrong with your taste-buds. That yellow thing is more than likely a bar of soap. Not the stuff that cheese omelettes are made of (and I'm not referring to egg).

Who invented soap? I only wish I knew. After all, people haven't always washed, have they? I doubt very much that the Ancient Britains washed very much. I can't imagine Danish Marauders getting the tin tub out in front of the fire every Friday night, can you? Although a nice long soak in the tub is just the thing after a long day's pillaging, I would have thought. Even in Regency times, people had to carry around pomanders full of sweet-smelling flowers, to disguise the pong of BO. Soap is made from animal fats. So, if you want to do your bit for conservation, give up washing! **(SEE ALSO: BEAUTY WITHOUT CRUELTY, BODY ODOUR, ENDANGERED SPECIES)**

SPEAKER – HOUSE OF COMMONS: JOB OPPORTUNITY *(Spee-cur: Howsov Comonz: Gob-opper Tune-Itty):* Another one of those great dressing-up jobs, although the choice of colour is limited to black. It would suit a Gothic, probably, although they might have to tone down their hairstyle in order to get it under the wig. The major drawback to the job is that you have to have previously been a politician, preferably one that no one has heard of. The big plus, though, is that you would be the only person in the country allowed to tell Mrs Thatcher off, and get paid for it! Even the Queen can't do that! **(SEE ALSO: POLITICIAN, QUEEN, GETTING A JOB)**

SPORT *(Spawt):* There is nothing wrong with sport for those who like that sort of thing. Personally I don't, as I've never been any good at it. I'm not even particularly good at watching it, mainly, I think, because most sports are more fun to play than to watch. Unlike capital punishment: it's probably more fun to watch a firing squad than it is to stand in front of one. **(SEE ALSO: GETTING OUT OF GAMES)**

SPOTS *(Spotz): See* ZITS. Do you realize that one of the things that you will be prevented from doing if you suffer from chronic Acne is joining the army? It's true, although I don't understand why. I mean, just because you've got spots is no reason to assume that you are a bad shot. In fact, I would have thought that having Acne would be an advantage. Instant camouflage: "Don't waste your bullets. That's not a Squaddie. It's an Eccles Cake!" **(SEE ALSO: ACNE, PLUKES)**

STAMP COLLECTING: HOBBY *(Stamp-Col-Ek-Ting: Hob-ee):* In simple terms, the collecting of stamps and sticking them into a book. A fairly easy hobby to get into, it can be made easier by becoming a Postman. Then you can ask your customers for the stamps off their letters. Or, if you fancy supplementing your income as well, you can take the stamps off *before* you deliver the letters, then tell your customers that, since there is no stamp, they will have to pay the postage. You'll make a fortune in no time at all. You'll also find that stamp collecting will help pass the time in prison. **(SEE ALSO: HOBBIES, COIN COLLECTING, ETC.)**

STREETWISE: EXPRESSION *(Strete-Wize: X-Preshun):* Trendy term meaning "to know your way around". Know where you're At, and where you're Going. If you'd like to be more Streetwise than you are, get a map. **(SEE ALSO: WHERE YOU'RE AT, WHERE YOU'RE COMING FROM)**

SUN *(Sunn):* Has all the outward signs of being a newspaper. In fact, it's the only newspaper capable of being read by Rottweilers. But apparently they don't bother. They think it lacks thrusting political comment, and the crossword is too hard. **(SEE ALSO: ROTTWEILERS, POSERS, FAME)**

SWEAT *(Swet):* It's a little known fact that the human body sweats one-and-a-half plastic lemonade bottles full of sweat a day. And, in hot weather this goes up to as much as two-and-a-half bottles. (Although I suppose it does depend on the size of the human body.) Now, I accept that this is a fact. What I *would* like to know is *how* do they know? How did they collect the sweat? Did they, for instance, strap plastic pop bottles up people's armpits for a day? Or did they go around the restaurants, wringing out the waiters' vests at closing time? And why pop bottles? Isn't that rather dangerous? Especially *lemonade* bottles! Could *you* tell the difference between lemonade and sweat? Without tasting it, I mean. It all sounds rather tricky to me. Still, I suppose that it's in the name of science. Cheers! Bottoms up! Lovely! Just the thing to wash down a school dinner! **(SEE ALSO: SCHOOL DINNERS)**

T

TAKE-AWAY FOOD: WHAT IS IT? *(Tayk-A-way-Fude: Wotizzit?):* It would be much easier for me to explain what it *isn't*. And it isn't the real thing. But then a Take-Away doesn't really *need* to taste like real food. Because you're going to eat it somewhere other than where you bought it, which means that the chances of your taking it back to complain about it are several million to one. And even if you do, they can always say:

> "Ah yes, but you took it out into the street, didn't you? Well, it's not designed for that, you see. And I expect you drove it home, did you? Oh, on your bike, eh? Oh, dear! You have to understand that the delicate balance of herbs and spices that go together to create the distinctive flavour of this particular dish is so fine that even the shortest cycle ride can upset it. What's more, unless my nose deceives me, I think you've sprinkled salt on it!"

By the time they've finished, you're almost offering to pay double for it!

The same cannot be said, however, for burgers and other so-called Fast Food. Your average Burger contains enough preservatives to give it a shelf-life of 126 years. So therefore you could buy a burger and fries (posh word for chips), take them home, pop them on a shelf, get married, raise a family, give your daughter's hand away in marriage, give the rest of her away in marriage, watch your grandchildren grow, and leave the burger and fries to one of them in your will – on the understanding that they take it back to the place you bought it from and complain that it was cold. The burger and chips would still be fresh and edible, and the fellow in the Take-Away would have no alternative but to give them their money back (or rather, *your* money back), by which time the price of the burger would probably have risen by several thousand per cent. Now, *that's* what you call an investment. (Mind you, I think that the ten-inch thick mould on the chips might give the game away, assuming the Take-Away guy noticed it!) (**SEE ALSO: SCHOOL DINNERS, EATING OUT**)

TALLER: HOW TO BE *(Tor-ler: How-2B):* There is sadly no simple straightforward way of becoming taller, other than by growing. It could be that, like me, you come from a long (or rather short) line of not very tall people. If so, then it's as likely as not that you too will be short. Incidentally, none of the old wives' tales, like sticking horse muck in your shoes, work. You just end up with very smelly socks and a following of champion rhubarb growers. But there is a simple way of becoming taller, although it does involve a bit of practice. I refer to the tying of a couple of tin-cans to your feet. Obviously it makes walking a bit tricky at first, and dancing is virtually impossible, but if it makes you look taller, it could be worth it. There are a few discos around the country that don't allow people in if they've got tin-cans tied to their feet, notably:

Doggs at Scunthorpe, Staggers at Widdlecombe Bay, Hamster Muggers in Stockport, Boyyos in Rhyll, Nerds in Ramsgate*, and Cobblers on the Isle of Mull.

Oh, and of course you'd also be refused entry to the Royal Festival Ballet and the Household Cavalry. But it might be worth it as you'll certainly meet a taller class of person.

This is a change of policy for Nerds, because at one time they'd let anyone in who knew what a tie was. This was to keep out members of the Armed Forces.* (SEE ALSO: DISCOS, POSERS, IMPRESSING YOUR DATE**)

TEACHERS: WHY ARE THEY SO GRUMPY? *(Teecherz: wye-R-thay-so Grumpie):* It is really unfair to generalize, isn't it. But all teachers without exception are grumpy. Not all the time. Just 90 per cent of it. But there is a very good reason. Which is the fact that they never stop going to School. They attend School as kids, then they go to University, then to Teacher Training College, then back to School. No wonder they're fed up. I mean, we think we have it bad just having to go to School until we're sixteen, but they are stuck with it for life! **(SEE ALSO: SCHOOL)**

TELEPHONIST: JOB OPPORTUNITY *(Tell EffonisT: Gob-Opper Tune-Itty):* The major quality required for this job, apart from the ability to pick up a phone, is tact. Try this simple test:

Someone phones up to speak to your Boss. Your Boss says: "Tell him that the only way I want to talk to him is through a medium!" Do you tell the Caller:

(A) "Mr Jackson is rather busy at the moment. Can I get him to call you back in about half an hour?" Or:
(B) "Mr Jackson says he's not here."

If the answer is (A) you could be in with a chance. Unless, of course, you've just been sacked. In which case, plump for (B)! **(SEE ALSO: RECEPTIONIST, GETTING A JOB)**

THAT'S MY BAG, MAN: EXPRESSION *(Th-atz-mi Bag Mann: X-Preshun):* This is basically a really cool and trendy way of saying: "Excuse me, mister, but I think that you've just picked up the wrong shopping."

THESAURUS: WHAT IS IT? *(Thees-or-us: Wotizzitt?):* Basically it's a dictionary of words with similar meanings, which enables you to say exactly the same thing in many different ways. Great if you're given to repeating yourself. It is just one of a host of different forms of dictionary. For example, there are also:

Bronte-saurus: A dictionary full of the kind of words you will need to know in order to write books such as *Jane Eyre*.

Tirana-saurus: A dictionary crammed with long unwieldy outdated words which will enable you to make the simplest thing sound amazingly complicated and boring (**SEE ALSO: JEFFREY ARCHER**)

Stagga-saurus: A very large dictionary that is almost impossible to carry without falling over. Usually called *The Pocket Edition.* (**SEE ALSO: SHAKESPEARE**)

TOURING WITH YOUR BAND/GROUP *(Tor-ing-withyor-Banned Grupe):* Touring with a pop band can be a real pain, particularly in the early days. Obviously, once you've Made It, as they say, you'll be staying in hotel rooms with more TV sets than you could possibly throw through the window, even if you stayed up all night. But when you're first starting out, you'll all have to bed down in the back of the van. That's if you've got a van. If not you might all have to try and squeeze into the saddle-bags on the bass-player's moped. It will be at times like this that you'll wish you'd taken my advice about having someone in the band with wealthy, generous parents. It'll also be at times like this that you'll wish you'd taken more care about naming your band.

Imagine it: you're playing the gig. You're going a storm, so much so that you are persuaded to play a few extra encores. When you come off stage you are all naturally starving. After all, you didn't get anything to eat before the show (well you did, but nerves brought it back up again!). You're starving, but there are no restaurants open (this means it could be as late as half-past eight in some provincial towns!). Anyway, just as you're all wondering what to do, your host at the venue (or more likely the caretaker) suddenly announces, surprise, surprise, they have laid on a meal. The unfortunate thing is that they had assumed, from your name (The Three Somethings) that there were only three of you. Not the 27 hungry mouths they now see salivating before them. Even a caretaker can't make three plates of food spread around 27 people. And certainly not 27 musicians, which is equivalent to 180 ordinary people. There has only ever been one person who could do that with food, and even though He is planning a second coming, it's unlikely to be at a mid-week gig of a little-known 27-piece Hip-Hop band called The Three Somethings. So, I suppose the lesson to learn from this is: if you are a 27-piece Hip-Hop band, and you insist on calling yourselves The Three

Somethings, take sandwiches. (**SEE ALSO: FORMING A BAND, POSERS, NAMING YOUR BAND**)

TRAIN SPOTTING *(Trane-Spot-In):* One of the simplest, and more rewarding, hobbies you can take up. It basically consists of standing on or near a railway station, near (but not *on*) a railway line, and Spotting trains, ie: seeing them. You need to keep a written record of the trains you have spotted, as the numbers on the trains have anything up to ten digits, and you could easily start to forget which ones you've seen after a few years. It can make for riveting conversations, I can tell you, especially now that very few trains actually have names, only numbers:

> *You:* You know what I spotted today? I spotted DN5677432B.
> *Someone else:* Get away!

I expect you can easily see how someone could get all fired up about the subject, can't you? But don't get too over-excited, because remember, railway lines are dangerous places. This Hobby is particularly popular with Anoraxics and Folksingers. (**SEE ALSO; ANORAXIA, FOLK MUSIC**)

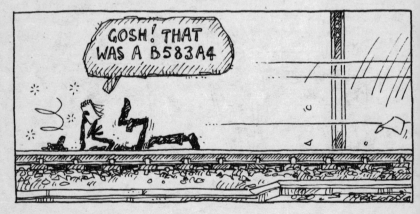

134

TUNING YOUR UKELELE *(chew-Ning Yor Yewker-lay-lee):* From time to time throughout this book I have given you information and advice which will clearly enrich the quality of your life. This is one such occasion. Knowing how to tune a ukelele is one of those truly useful bits of knowledge that break through language barriers, and establish you as an intellectual giant. So, how is it done? Very, very easily, but I suggest that you keep that to yourself. All you need is a Uke (as we say in the Muz Biz) and you're more than half-way there. Hold the Uke in the usual Uke-holding position, and then say: "My dog has fleas", plucking a different string for each word. You'll notice that there are four words, and a Uke has four strings, unless there are some missing. Once you have said: "My dog has fleas", and plucked each of the strings, you'll find that the Uke is tuned. This is what *I* always do, anyway. One of my deepest regrets is that I've never really got very far, despite my obvious talent on the Uke. I've never really understood why. (SEE ALSO: LEARNING AN INSTRUMENT, FORMING A BAND)

TURN-ON *(Ter-Non):* Switch on, start up. Often used in connection with making a cup of tea, as in "Turn on the Kettle". Has been used in a sexual context, but this is obviously silly. There's nothing very sexy about a cup of tea. Although I suppose it does depend on how you make it. (SEE ALSO: LOVE)

TV PRESENTER (CHILDREN'S): JOB OPPORTUNITY *(Tee-Vee Prez-Enter (Chill-drenz): Gob-opper Tune-Itty):* Anyone can become a TV Presenter. There is absolutely no skill required. This is something that you will already have been aware of, I'm sure. In fact, I imagine that you have often sat in front of the TV, watching one of the latest rash* of Presenters, and thinking: I could do that. And I'm sure you could. But, you must be honest when you ask yourself: Have I got what it takes? So, what *does* it take, exactly? I'll tell you:

Youth: Or at least the appearance of youth. If you look more than 13½, forget it.

Regional Accent: In the interests of giving the impression that the programmes are for everyone, even people who live north of Watford, the Powers That Be in Medialand decree that their young presenters should have a regional accent. That is to say that they should either come from somewhere other than London, or be able to do a funny voice that makes them sound as though they do. Scottish is very popular at the moment. As is a sort of All-Purpose Northern. Liverpool, of course, is always popular, because everyone knows that, if you come from Liverpool, you're a *bundle of laughs*, despite the poverty, the violence, and the visits from the Prince of Wales. Oh, Welsh is a bit of a non-starter, although Irish is OK, although it helps if you sound like Gloria Hunniford, but look much much much younger, which shouldn't present too much of a problem.

Speech Defect: Now, here we are not talking about the sort of thing that makes people who watch *Allo Allo* wet themselves. The sort of speech impediment that is always popular with the Big Boys of Medialand is a slight lisp or a weak R. Anything that can sound "Cute". So, if you have such a thing, and are worried about it, you needn't be. You can always become a TV Presenter. And when you get too old to be one of these, you can become a Politician.

Energy: Very important quality. The average TV Presenter is required to *enthuse* about absolutely everything, without fear or favour. If you're called upon to present an item out of doors, particularly if this is also in front of a Live audience, then you will be required to jump about as much as possible. The more this jumping about is totally random the better, as it always looks *great* if you keep jumping out of camera shot, and the cameraman has to jump about to keep up with you. Mind you, the cameraman may have something to say about this after the show. (**SEE ALSO: BUNCH OF FIVES, SELF DEFENCE**)

Puppets: The current trend is for TV Presenters not to work alone. Currently they each work alongside a puppet. Sometimes it's really hard to work out which is which. Usually the puppet is the sensible one. Now, there's an old saying: "Never work with children or animals." But puppets don't seem to mind. They'll work with anyone.

So, having gone through these basic requirements, do you still feel *Person* enough to be a TV Presenter (Children's)? If you do – well: Fetch It! (sorry! I mean Go For It!)

*Rash: I used this word earlier, because that's another must for a Young TV presenter: Zits! (**SEE ALSO: TV PRESENTER SUPER-LATIVES, ZITS, POSERS**)

TV PRESENTER SUPERLATIVES *(Tee-Vee Prez-Enter Soup-er-latt-ivz):* All TV Presenters, from Quiz Show Hosts like Bob Monkhouse (Yes! That's what he is! Honest!), to linkmen like Andy Crane, need a full repertoire of Superlatives. Words like: Brilliant! Amazing! Brill! Super! Fantastic! Incredible! Unbelievable! etc. A really good TV Presenter, if there ever is one, will be able to combine several of these to create an even more meaningless superlative, such as, Amazingly-Superbrilliant! Personally, I can hardly wait! (**SEE ALSO: POSERS, ROTTWEILERS, SCHOOL: POINT OF**)

U

UGLY: AM I? *(Ug-Lee: Ameye?):* Probably. (SEE ALSO: BODY ODOUR, BAD BREATH, DOCTOR, DENTIST)

UNISEX HAIRDRESSING: STARTING YOUR OWN BUSINESS *(Yoo-knee-Sekz hare-dressin: Star-Ting Yorone Biz-Niz):* Once you've started hairdressing, it'll take you no time at all to save enough money to start your own business. After all, everyone needs their hair cut, you can charge as much as you like (although you must provide extras like coffee), and the hours you'll be working are so long you won't have any time to spend your earnings. So, logically, you'll be able to save your wages. The first thing you'll need are premises – somewhere to cut people's hair. Many hairdressers go to their clients' homes, but this can prove expensive if you don't drive, and tiring on a skateboard. Pick an empty shop that people are used to visiting. A condemned Oxfam Shop is perfect. Oxfam Shops are constantly full of little old ladies, and little old ladies like having their hair cut (actually they like the coffee and the chat more than anything). Also, little old ladies make very good customers for the young hairdresser, particularly short-sighted little old ladies. Little old men are a different matter. I doubt that you will be able to persuade them to visit your Unisex Salon. They prefer a good old-fashioned barber, preferably Italian.

Having got your premises, stripped it back to basics, installed your stereo (most important), wash basins (less important), and mirrors (very risky unless you actually know what you're doing), the next thing to do is to make it look *IMPRESSIVE*. This can be done by adding a few posters from the Shampoo Rep, and leaving little piles of hair around the floor. Oh, and if you can get someone, it doesn't really matter who, to attend one of those haircare courses, you'll be able to hang a Certificate of Attendance on the wall. You've probably seen the sort of thing: "This is to Certify that Tracy Skoggins attended a twenty-minute lecture on 'Washing Hair Without Disturbing the Head-Lice'". No one ever reads these certificates, but they always look very flash. You see. Image is everything.

Another very good way to look impressive is to have several

girls (preferably called Stacey, Sharon or Karon) with very outlandish hairstyles (Wigs will do) and loud piercing voices, to hang around the wash basins, get in everyone's way, talk about their boyfriends' naughty-bits and giggle a lot. That way all your customers will know that your salon is The Real Thing. You see, it is all about creating the right environment. Just as Doctors have to fill their waiting-rooms with very old magazines with little or nothing between their covers, so Hairdressers have to fill their salons with very young girls with little or nothing between their ears. Oh. One final word of warning. Try to avoid using those big old-fashioned hair driers that go over the client's head. No one ever remembers that the customer is under there until the screaming has stopped and the paramedics have got her on a ventilator. Remember, you want your customers to come back. Or, if they can't, at least to have passed your salon's telephone number on to their next-of-kin.

V

VEGGIES *(Vedgyz):* These days people are beginning to feel more and more that eating meat, and using animals to produce cosmetics and so on, is wrong. Of course, in some cases people just pay lip service to the issue, but this lip service doesn't extend to their lips stopping meat from getting past and into their stomachs. Some people, on the other hand, opt for total abstention from using animal products. These are called Vegans. Then there are the ones who try to avoid cosmetics made with animal fats, and don't eat meat. These are called Vegetarians. There are those who don't eat meat, but do eat fish, arguing presumably that a fish is not an animal. These are called Not Very Bright Vegetarians. Then there are the ones who avoid all animal products, including leather shoes, campaign vigorously for animal rights, and never ever eat any meat, fish or dairy products, unless of course there's nothing else in the fridge. These are called Complete Rodneys. **(SEE ALSO: BEAUTY WITHOUT CRUELTY)**

VESTS: WHY DO WAITERS WEAR THEM? *(Vestz: Y-Doo-way-Terz-where-thum?):* The simple answer is Sweat. Being a waiter is a very sweaty business. Really! This is because they move so fast. Now, obviously you are going to find this hard to believe, particularly if you've ever waited three hours for a glass of water (I know a restaurant where the service is so slow, that I always make a point of asking if I can order from tomorrow's menu!) So how do the waiters work up such a sweat? The kitchens. They are very hot. And while you are waiting for your meal, the waiter is doing the thing that the job-title suggests, waiting in the kitchen. Getting sweaty. This is why they wear a vest. Because customers don't like sweat dripping in their food. Waiters know this because several people have told them so: "Waiter, there's some soup in my sweat!" And so they wear vests. And so that you know that they are wearing a vest, they wear a very thin shirt over it, so that you can clearly see the vest through it (although I do know eating houses where they just wear the vest). And they move very slowly, like fashion models, so that you get a good look at their vest. This is something I feel sure you will find very reassuring. (**SEE ALSO: SWEAT, EATING OUT**)

VISIT TO THE DOCTOR'S: A *(Vizzi-too the Dock-ters a):* When going to the doctor's, try to make sure that there's something wrong with you. Going to the doctor's simply to get out of the rain, or because you've just learned a new magic trick and need someone to try it out on is not likely to make you very popular. Particularly with people who are really ill. Unless, of course, you're very old. The 1982 National Health Act allows for "Persons of an old, decrepid, or crumbly nature, to visit, sit in, or otherwise occupy (except by military force) a doctor's surgery, or similar establishment set up for the distribution of drugs (not including Discos or Acid House Parties)" (**SEE ALSO: DISCOS, ACID HOUSE PARTIES, DRINK AND DRUGS**). The only other way you will be welcome at a health centre without a health defect is if you are a Private Patient. Under another section of the same 1982 Act, a Private Patient has all the same rights as an old person, plus he/she may "enter the doctor's consulting room, call him by his first name and have a go with his stethoscope". This does not, unfortunately, include members of BUPA. But it sounds almost worth going private, doesn't it?

If you have got a legitimate complaint, telephone for an appointment. This should reduce your waiting time at the surgery quite considerably. Down to just a few days, in fact. Take something to eat during your wait. Most surgeries allow sandwiches, and maybe a thermos, but they draw the line at Primas stoves or open wood fires. A sleeping bag is also quite a good idea, although most doctor's surgeries are full of old newspaper, and this makes a perfectly adequate bed. If your complaint is *personal*, do not, whatever you do, take your Mum or Dad with you. It'll be all round the family in five minutes. You might just as well take a *Sun* journalist and photographer in there!

One final word of warning: if you feel unwell, do not hesitate to contact the doctor. He is there to help you. If you have checked in the *Reader's Digest Book of Terminal Illnesses*, and discovered that you only have half an hour to live, phone the doctor straight away. Don't wait until you've watched *Neighbours*. Although, on second thoughts, watching it may take your mind off your own dire state by making you realize that there are lots of people worse off than you. The whole cast of *Neighbours*, for example! (SEE ALSO: AUSTRALIAN, RECEP-TIONIST, GETTING A JOB)

VOX-POPS: WHAT ARE THEY? *(Vox-popz: Wot-R-thay?):* You've probably seen programmes, or newsreels, where Ordinary people are interviewed in the street. Occasionally they are asked their opinion on something (they often say "don't know"), but usually they are given different foods or drinks to sample, or, in the case of something like *That's Life*, they are asked to make Complete Rodneys of themselves. Without getting paid! That's terrible! I mean, it's OK for the person with the "mike" (Medialand jargon for microphone), because they are paid vast sums of money to look incredibly stupid. In fact, it's precisely because they *do* look incredibly stupid that they got the job in the first place! (SEE ALSO: TV

PRESENTER (CHILDREN'S)), but, anyway, I'm sure you've seen them. If you haven't, then you've evidently just arrived from the planet Zlomph. So, may I bid you a warm welcome to Earth. I hope you come in peace and that your stay will be a happy one. (**SEE ALSO: VOX POPS, POSERS**)

VOX-POPS: HOW TO GET INTO ONE *(Vox-popz: Howe-2-gettin-21):* This should be incredibly easy, as there are at least two happening in every street at any given time. Well there are, unless you live in somewhere like Buxton, or Scunthorpe. It's not your fault, but your Mr Average TV Producer has never heard of you or your town. He only got to hear about Berkshire because his accountant advised him to buy it so that he wouldn't have to pay so much tax (**SEE ALSO: ACCOUNTANT**). But, if you live within a few miles of a TV station, you are very likely to be approached in the street and asked your opinion on either (a) the state of the world, or (b) the forkful of something that looks as if it's come out of one or other end of a hamster, and is currently being pushed up your nose. At least, you will be approached if you fulfil the criteria. You will be passed by on the other side, if you are not either:

(A) *Called Tracy*: Or something that mediafolk regard as equally common. You see, the interviewees must appear to be every inch the Ordinary Person in the Street. (It helps if they're also giggly).

(B) *Old*: This is another quality that goes down well with mediafolk. But just being Old isn't enough. The old person must also be Totally Uninhibited. A degree of madness is a real bonus, because this usually means that the old person will not have a clue what's going on, and suddenly break into one of those wonderful old songs that made Britain great (or should that be Grate?), and helped us through two World Wars. They will only be stopped from singing when they have removed most of their clothing.

By now you are probably becoming very depressed, as you realize that your chances of being in one of these Vox Pops is very slim. After all, you are a real person, and therefore of no interest to the Mediafolk, who are looking for people who are ordinary in a completely extraordinary way. Of course, they do interview Schoolkids, but only if they look as though they've just come straight from appearing on Crime Watch. So, what can you do?

Well, there are several ways of ensuring that you get your face On Television. Standing in the Back of Shot (ie: behind the person being interviewed) is usually a good way, as long as you wave, pull faces and generally make a total Wally of yourself. However, TV crews are getting wise to this, and tend to film their interviewee pressed up against a wall (or nailed to a tree), so that no one can sneak in behind. What I would suggest would be a Diversion. Something that takes the viewers' eyes totally off the interview and on to you. Bank Robbery, Mugging, Streaking, Rampaging through an Arndale Centre with a fireman's axe – none of these will work. What you need to do is something totally unexpected and out of the ordinary. For example, you could just smile and say "Hallo" to someone, in a perfectly friendly and neighbourly way. That will really cause the heads to turn. (**SEE ALSO: IMPRESSING YOUR DATE**)

W

WACKY: EXPRESSION *(Wak-Eee: X-preshun):* Another one of those Media-generated words, meaning . . . well, meaning Wacky, really! Of course, as you might suspect, it can give you a potentially high score in Scrabble (K=4, Y=4, W=4). **(SEE ALSO: GREAT SCRABBLE CONSPIRACY)**

WAITERS: ATTRACTING THE ATTENTION OF *(Way-terz: At-rack-ting thee a-10-shunov):* Not an easy thing to do at the best of times, but it can be done. It depends on what you want to attract their attention for. Different things call for different measures. Just trying to get served is virtually impossible, unless you are actually related to the waiter concerned, and even then he will only acknowledge you if you

owe him money. Often a way around this is to get a school or college friend to get a job at your favourite eatery, then offer to do their homework, in return for a look at the menu. This could backfire, by making you too busy to go out to eat at all! But, if you choose not to take this course, and you'd be wise not to, then more desperate measures may be called for.

Setting fire to the table can usually be guaranteed to get you a glass of water. However, make sure that you've got your mouth open when it arrives, as it is almost certainly going to be thrown over you. The only sure way of attracting the waiter's attention is to shoot yourself, then, when he asks if you would like him to call you an ambulance, you say: "Yes, please. Oh, and could I order a meal while I'm waiting?" This plan has the added bonus of your not having to sit around waiting for a meal to arrive. You can go off to hospital, spend a week recovering amid flowers and fruit, then get back to the restaurant in good time to eat. In fact, you may only then have to wait as little as twenty minutes. (**SEE ALSO: VESTS, HOSPITAL FOOD, SWEAT**)

WALKMAN *(Wor-k-Mann):* When the art of conversation died in the mid-seventies, mainly because people were afraid to speak to each other in case they got their faces punched, many people found themselves at a loss as to what to do with themselves, when they were walking along the road. They had always been used to saying, "Hallo" to passers-by, and generally behaving like characters in *Postman Pat*. Suddenly this harmless pastime was denied them. At home, of course, there was no problem. TV had already replaced the art of conversation, and no one missed it. But no one had yet thought of carrying TV along the road with them. Then some bright Spark (Media-speak for electrician) hit on the idea of a small stereo system that ran off batteries, with mini head-phones that either fitted inside the ear, damaging your ear-drum, or sat on the outside of the ear, thus allowing the

REGGAE

IRISH
DANCE
MUSIC

CLASSICAL

RUSSIAN

rest of the world to know that you were listening to Barry Manilow. But this invention revolutionized walking, and was soon followed by the Personal CD Player, the Personal TV and the Cellular phone. It's strange, isn't it, that although the use of Walkmans is now so widespread . . . just a minute, should that be Walk*men*? Or, in the interests of sexual equality, should it perhaps be Walk*people*? Anyway, it is strange that no one has yet come up with a term meaning: The Using of Personal Stereos. Well, what about "Walkmanship"? Sounds good. Has the right amount of pretentious meaninglessness to ensure that it will get picked up by the Media. There is a school of thought that would argue that the best word to use to describe the playing of a Personal Stereo would be Annoying. But this is because they are on the outside listening in. They are the victims of Passive Walkmanship. Some people really are irrationally anti-Walkmans, aren't they? Is this because they are ex-Walkman users? You know, in the same way ex-smokers become very anti-smoking? I am very tolerant of Walkmanship, probably because I am a Walkman user myself.

In fact, with Walkmanship, you can often tell what music people are listening to by the way they walk. (SEE ALSO: DISCOS, ACID HOUSE PARTIES, REGGAE)

WANNA-BEES *(Wonner-beez):* A Medialand expression. It's probably been around for years, but it got used to death when Madonna first rose to fame. It was used to describe girls who, apparently, wanted to be Madonna (or rather *wann'ed* to be Madonna). The expression drifted into obscurity when the Media realized that these girls didn't actually wanna *be* Madonna. They just Wann-ed to *have* Madonna's *cash*!

WAR *(Worrrr):* Traditionally a way of settling an argument, when offering a Bunch of Fives fails. The only real difference is that it is usually someone else's argument. (SEE ALSO: ROTT-WEILERS, BUNCH OF FIVES, QUEEN, SELF DEFENCE, GODS)

WHERE YOU'RE AT: EXPRESSION
(Wear-yor-at: X-Preshun): Trendy way of saying where you are at the moment. Destination. (**SEE ALSO: POSERS, TV PRESENTERS (CHILDREN'S)**)

WHERE YOU'RE COMING FROM: EXPRESSION *(Wear-yor-cumming-from: X-Preshun):* Original position. Presumably where you start out from in order to get where you're eventually at. Often said by Person A to Person B, when Person A has already been where Person B is now, and Person B is shortly to join Person A where *they* are now. Hence Person A would say: "I know where you're coming from", and Person B would reply: "I know where you're at", which is just as well, otherwise they would never meet up, and that would be a tragedy, because they would never get to continue their riveting conversation.

Where you're at

Where you're coming from

WHY DO YOU NEVER GET A PLUG? *(Wye-dooyoo neffa-getta-Plugg?):* To date the number of electrical goods that you have bought may be quite small: Stereo, train-set, hair drier, electrolysis machine for the hamster. But, as life winds on, and you get into food processors, drills, TVs, videos and all the trappings of Family Life, you will become more and more aware of the fact that British electrical goods never have plugs! Now, you may wonder why this is. I will tell you. Or, at least, I will pass on the explanation that I was given when I bought a new toaster and the salesperson said: "Do you want a plug?"

What a strange thing to say! Perhaps they thought that I wasn't actually going to plug it in, but just leave it sitting on the breakfast bar, so that passers-by could admire it and say: "Ah! I see you've got a toaster".

"Yes, I have. You're right. I'm seriously thinking of getting a plug for it, but, well, you never know where that sort of thing is going to lead, do you?"

"Quite."

Anyway, I got a plug, and then asked why British electrical goods never have them. I was told: "*It's because foreign plugs are different.*"

Now, I assume that the salesperson thought that I might want to do my toasting abroad somewhere, even though the toast would clearly be cold by the time I got back home with it. "Won't be long, darling. Just popping over to Tuscany to do a spot of toasting. Pop the kettle on. I'll be back before you can recite the Koran." I realize that you don't have to win *Mastermind* to work in a shop, but if a simple thing like a customer needing a plug confuses them, perhaps they're in the wrong job! (SEE ALSO: UNISEX HAIRDRESSING, GETTING A JOB).

WICKED: EXPRESSION *(Wick-Ed: X-Preshun):* A word meaning *bad, debased, evil, sinful, vile* and *worthless*. In more recent times it has been used to mean amazing! brilliant! (wacky, zany, etc). In fact there was a Saturday morning TV show called *It's Wicked!* (I wonder whether it was named after the new meaning of "wicked", or the original meaning?) But Wicked is a good word, and – surprise, surprise – a high Scrabble scorer! (SEE ALSO: GREAT SCRABBLE CONSPIRACY)

WIMBLEDON *(Wimble-Don):* On the face of it this is just an innocent annual tennis tournament. But it is in fact another part of the sinister plot to Stop Children watching TV. (SEE ALSO: CRICKET, SNOOKER) Also, because the tournament is held in England, the English never win it. This is because we consider it impolite to beat our visitors. It has nothing to do with a lack of ability. This attitude also explains why we have always fought our wars abroad, and why, on the few occasions that anyone has fought us on English soil (Normans, Danes), we've let them win. It doesn't explain why we hardly ever win the World Cup, since it is rarely played in Britain. In fact, that particular failure has become so embarrassing, that groups of very patriotic supporters are doing their level best to get us banned from it for ever, thus avoiding any further embarrassment. (**SEE ALSO: SPORT, FOOTBALL, DISCOS, SELF DEFENCE, ROTTWEILERS, PUNK, GETTING OUT OF GAMES**)

X

X-RATED FILMS *(X-ray tidfilmz):* When I was a child, all films had to have a certificate from the British Board of Film Censors. Any film that didn't get a certificate was either cut, changed or not shown in public. The gradings were:

U: Which meant anyone could watch it. Anyone, that is, with the money to get in, and the height to reach the pay window.

A: Children under fourteen not admitted, unless accompanied by an adult. This adult was generally regarded as having to be one or other of their parents, or a total stranger who could be persuaded to play surrogate dad for five minutes, until you and all your mates were inside

the cinema. Mind you, as there tended to be about six of you and since you were all roughly the same age, this got the volunteer father some very strange looks from the ticket lady: "D'you know, your family is the 48th case of unidentical sextuplets we've had in here this week!"

AA: Children under fourteen not admitted unless accompanied by a member of a motoring association.

X: The forbidden one, and the one you always tried to get to see. The rating meant no one under 18 was admitted, but you were a King at school if you'd managed to get in to see an "X" film. Especially if you were still in infant school. If you *did* manage to get to see an "X", the trick was not to be too boastful, but to play it very casual. Oh, and never ever admit that you hadn't understood a word of it!

The ratings these days have changed, as have the meanings:

U: Anyone who can be bothered to can watch it.

PG, 12, 15, 18: Wait until it comes out on video.

(SEE ALSO: KISSING: WHEN?, KISSING: HOW?)

Y

YOU ARE WHAT YOU EAT *(Yoo-R-Wotu-Eeet):* Someone once said: "You are what you eat." This can't be true. I mean I can't believe that Russell Grant has ever eaten a beached whale. **(SEE ALSO: RUSSELL GRANT, BONNIE LANGFORD, BRANDRETH, JEFFREY ARCHER, RANTZEN)**

OH DEAR MY LITTLE BROTHER HAS BEEN EATEN BY THE PIRANHAS I BOUGHT HIM FOR CHRISTMAS AND ACCIDENTALLY LEFT IN THE BATH

YOUNGER BROTHERS: LEGALLY DISPOSING OF *(Yun-Ger Bruth-Erz: Lea-glee Dis-Posi-Ing of):* It is not as easy as it used to be. Parents have become more sophisticated. This is because we let them watch too much Television. And once they get a Satellite dish, who *knows* how sophisticated they might become? But the up-shot of all this is that Parents no longer fall for the old The Killer Hamsters Have Done Away With My Beloved Brother routine. So, there's really nothing for it – you may have to get a Rottweiler. One that's particularly *fond* of younger brothers. **(SEE ALSO: ROTTWEILERS, PARENTS)**

YOUR OWN DISCO: RUNNING *(Yorown-Diss-co: Ru-Ning):* Putting your own disco together could not be easier. Well, actually, it could. But, if you've got a few hundred quid for the equipment, the gift of the gab and a copy of the *Birdie Song*, you should give it a go. Firstly, before you splash out loadsa money on equipment, decide what kind of audience you're hoping to play to. If it's people of your own age, then obviously you'll need a good range of records, all the chart sounds and plenty of dance music. You can, of course, get special Disco mixes, but these cost money. Anyone with a modest knowledge of electronics should be able to adjust the playing speed of the sound decks to suit Disco beat. You'll probably need twin decks unless you are either extremely fast at changing records, or you adjust the record speed so much that everyone needs a ten-minute rest between each disc.

For a young audience, lighting is also important. Or rather, a lack of it is. Young People prefer to dance in the dark, so as long as you've got a box of matches or a pen-torch in order to help you see to change the record, you'll be OK. Obviously, after a time, you'll get used to putting the record on in the dark, but you may go through a few embarrassing weeks of putting them on the turntable while they're still in their sleeves. Your customers may not notice, but it doesn't do the needle a lot of good. A knowledge of braille may be helpful here. It's something to bear in mind when you're considering your GCSE options with a view to planning your career.

But discos aren't all music. Oh, no! And it would be as well to remember this when you're planning your evening's entertainment. A few simple prizes would be a useful thing to take with you: individually wrapped cigarettes, bottles of Babycham for the ladies, that sort of thing. Remember, people don't only want to dance, so anything that brings an element of relaxed good humour into the proceedings would go down a treat. This is particularly true of older people because of heart conditions, but it works with all ages. You've probably seen the sort of thing I'm talking about at Wedding Discos. First person to reach the mike with a forged Barclay-card, the person with the knobbliest knees, dirtiest knickers etc. gets a prize. For Kiddies' Discos, a few simple magic tricks always go down well. But don't try sawing anyone in half unless you're insured. And remember, if all else fails – stick on the *Birdie Song*! (**SEE ALSO: DISCOS**)

Z

ZANY *(Zay-knee):* A totally meaningless word specially invented to describe very bad Children's Television Programmes. It was probably invented by a maker of very bad Children's Television Programmes. This person has probably never fathered, mothered or even met a child. If they had they would realize that Zany is not common usage for kids. It is, however, a word that scores very highly in Scrabble. Could this be why the word was invented? Quite possibly. Do you realize that Zany carefully placed in the corner of the board, with its "Z" on "Double Letter" and its "Y" on "Triple Word", scores a monstrous 78 Points! Worth selling your soul for, I would have thought. (**SEE ALSO: WACKY, GREAT SCRABBLE CONSPIRACY**)

ZAP *(Zapp):* Another one of those meaningless words. On the one hand it is what the old Batman used to do to his

158

enemies. It is also what Aliens From Other Planets do to people. Or so we're told. There is little or no evidence to support this. But the Powers That Be (that is to say: Hollywood Producers and Scrabble Champions) tell us that Aliens carry ray-guns and go about "zapping" everyone. Until someone goes to another galaxy and finds out differently, that's what everyone will believe. Well, I for one think that the scaremongers are going to look pretty silly when the first aliens land and, instead of "Zapping" everyone with little plastic ray-guns just like the ones in Toys-R-Us, they start inviting everyone to sleep-overs and barn dances. (**SEE ALSO: WACKY, DISCOS**)

ZITS *(Zitz):* Less attractive name for acne. Although, let's face it, there is little or nothing attractive about acne, whatever you

call it. It's there, staring you in the face. The only consolation is that it goes away, eventually. There are, of course, numerous potions on the market, all claiming to make your Zits disappear while you sleep. Oh yeah? Well, that's OK if you're prepared to go to bed for about five years. Very few of these potions actually work, but I suppose it gives you something to do while you wait for your spots to go. If you're keen to try any of these potions, what I suggest you do is this: Go into your nearest chemist's, and ask for the cheapest spot cream they sell. Also ask for a brown paper bag (you could say that you need the bag because you're too embarrassed to let people see what you've bought). Then, once outside the shop, throw the cream away and stick the bag on your head. Obviously cut some eyeholes in the bag, if you want to avoid an accident. On the other hand, if your spots embarrass you so much that you wish you were dead, don't bother with the eyeholes. (**SEE ALSO: PLUKES, SPOTS, ACNE, JEFFREY ARCHER**)